COMMUNITY COLLEGE EDUCATION AND ITS IMPACT ON SOCIOECONOMIC STATUS ATTAINMENT

COMMUNITY COLLEGE EDUCATION AND ITS IMPACT ON SOCIOECONOMIC STATUS ATTAINMENT

Elizabeth Monk-Turner

Mellen Studies in Education
Volume 41

The Edwin Mellen Press
Lewiston•Queenston•Lampeter

Library of Congress Cataloging-in-Publication Data

Monk-Turner, Elizabeth.
    Community college education and its impact on socioeconomic status attainment / Elizabeth Monk-Turner.
        p.   cm. -- (Mellen studies in education) ; v. 41)
    Includes bibliographical references (p.   ) and index.
    ISBN 0-7734-8253-9 (hard)
        1. Community colleges--United States--Sociological aspects.
    2. Community college students--United States--Social conditions.
    3. Community college students--United States--Economic conditions.
    4. Education, Higher--Social aspects--United States.   5. Education,
    Higher--Economic aspects--United States.   I. Title.   II. Series.
    LB2328. 15.U6M65   1998
    378.1'543--dc21   98-44215
                                                                        CIP

This is volume 41 in the continuing series
Mellen Studies in Education
Volume 41 ISBN 0-7734-8253-9
MSE Series ISBN 0-88946-935-0

A CIP catalog record for this book is available from the British Library.

The Edwin Mellen Press   The Edwin Mellen Press
        Box 450   Box 67
Lewiston, New York   Queenston, Ontario
USA 14092-0450   CANADA L0S 1L0

The Edwin Mellen Press, Ltd.
Lampeter, Ceredigion, Wales
UNITED KINGDOM SA48 8LT

Printed in the United States of America

To my husband, *Charlie Turner*

Table of Contents

Community Colleges in the Higher Educational System

Community colleges are two-year institutions of higher education. They are local in orientation and are geared to be responsive to changes in the local labor market. Today, community colleges emphasize career or vocational education programs leading to immediate employment. Junior colleges are two-year colleges geared almost exclusively to transfer. The junior college label, therefore, became increasingly inappropriate as greater stress was placed on vocational education in two-year colleges. Recognizing this change, the American Association of Junior Colleges changed its name to the American Association of Community and Junior Colleges in 1972. In my work, I use the terms two-year and community college interchangeably.

Some of the early supporters of community colleges were the presidents of elite universities, for example, Henry Tappan (University of Michigan), William Harper (University of Chicago), and David Jordan (Stanford University).[1] These educators wanted to establish the junior college as an institution separate from the university. They conceived of the two-year college as a transfer-oriented institution. Students would begin their higher education by attending a community college where they would acquire the first two years of their college education. Then advanced students would transfer and attend the university to specialize in a particular field.

The first two-year college, the Lewis Institute of Chicago, was established at the University of Chicago in 1896. The first two year Associate of Arts degree was granted by this institution several years later. Joliet College, established in Illinois in 1901, was the first independent junior college.[2] Joliet College was basically an extension of the secondary school system and was under the direct control of the local school board. Since the early 1900s governance of public two-year colleges has gradually changed from lower elementary and high school control to operation under separate junior college districts. Thus, community colleges have origins in both higher and secondary education and their financing contains elements of the financing of both.[3] Today most community colleges are financed at the local level. Such financing means that community college spending is tied to the revenue of the local community it serves. Recently, moves have been made to organize the administration of community colleges on the state rather than the local level.[4]   Educators who supported the development of two-year, transfer oriented institutions were not successful in establishing the community college as a separate institution where all entering college students took the first two years of a liberal arts education. Nevertheless, many of the first two-year colleges emphasized academic courses. Vocational training was not a major part of the curriculum. Occupational programs were first developed in two-year colleges after the passage of the Smith-Hughes vocational education legislation of the 1920s.[5] However, before World War II, fewer than 25 percent of community college students were in vocational programs. For most college students, getting a college education meant working toward a baccalaureate degree. A four-year college education helped prepare students to enter professional and managerial level jobs.

After World War II, community college enrollment soared. The GI Bill of Rights brought service people into the higher educational system. Many enrolled in community colleges. Vocational education was not new to them. Thus, the extension of vocational training to community colleges began to gain acceptance.[6] The changing structure of the economy helped create an atmosphere for a change of emphasis from a liberal arts education for everyone to the development of vocational programs to meet new needs. After the war, the composition of the labor force changed. Between 1950 and 1970, the proportion of technical workers in the labor force rose from 7.1 percent to 14.5 percent.[7] Higher education no longer had to be the same for everyone. Education could be different and equal too. It was during this post-war period that community colleges came to be called people's colleges.

Supporters emphasize that the mission of the community college is to facilitate social mobility. They see the community college as an institution open to all. It is a place where all individuals have an equal opportunity. Critics argue that community colleges are educational wastelands where students' aspirations are bridled and where many students are tracked into vocational programs. Critics argue that community college education is an extension of class-based tracking into higher education.[8] They also see the community college as an institution where working class people, people from disadvantaged ethnic and racial groups, and women are given a chance to try, as Pincus writes, not a chance to succeed. Critics argue that nontraditional community college students have, at best, an opportunity to obtain an education that will train them for positions roughly commensurate with their social origins.[9]

This work examines the role of the community college in the United States. Are community colleges an extension of a class-based tracking system in education or are they the avenues for upward mobility that their supporters claim? Researchers largely ignored this question, in part, because most available data did not distinguish educational experience by type of college entered. How community college education shapes adult income and occupational status is an important, yet neglected, area of analysis.

HISTORY OF COMMUNITY COLLEGE DEVELOPMENT

Since the early 1960s, the number of public two-year colleges in the United States has rapidly increased. The most rapid period of growth was between the early 1960s and the late 1970s. For example, in 1963, there were only 634 two-year colleges. By the late 1970s, this figure increased to 1,190 (an 88% increase). By 1978, there were twice as many public two-year colleges in the United States as public four-year colleges and institutions. As of 1995, this trend continues.

4

Currently, we have 1,284 public two year institutions (only 94 more than in 1978) and 629 public four-year institutions.[10]

ENROLLMENTS

Along with the rise in the number of institutions was an explosion in the number of students who began their higher education at a community college. In 1963, few (844,512) students were enrolled in two-year institutions. By 1985, 4,270,000 students were enrolled in public two-year institutions. Enrollment in two-year colleges doubled between the years 1970 and 1985, a change of 112 percent, while enrollment in four-year colleges increased by only 21 percent. Today, 48 percent of all students enrolled in higher education are at community colleges not four-year institutions.

Since 1977, enrollment for women has exceeded that for men in community colleges. Many vocational programs in the community college are directed towards women. These include: secretarial programs, health and paramedical technology programs, data processing technologies, education, home economics, and library science. The most likely fields for the Associate of Arts degree to be awarded to women, in 1991-92, were in secretarial or business data processing programs, nursing, or the visual and performing arts.[11]

Over half (53 percent) of female undergraduates were enrolled in public community colleges in 1988, compared with 48 percent of male undergraduates. Notably, in 1960, the majority (86 percent) of all women enrolled in higher education in the United States were in four-year colleges. Few (14 percent) entered community colleges. By 1988, over half (53 percent) of all women enrolled in higher education were in two-year colleges. The chances of a woman who attended college of entering a four-year college dropped from 86 percent to 47 percent over this time period.[12] How type of first college entered shapes life opportunities is critical given these changes in enrollment.

Minority students are more likely than white students to attend a community college. By 1988, 49 percent of African American students enrolled in college were enrolled in public two-year institutions (up 5 percent from 1976). Today more than half of all students with an American Indian/Alaskan Native (57%) or Hispanic (63%) background and almost half (49%) of all students with an Asian/Pacific Islander background enrolled in college are in public two-year institutions. In 1994, the majority (54 percent) of white students were enrolled in four-year colleges.[13]

COLLEGE QUALITY DIFFERENCES

The quality of the community college faculty is markedly lower than the quality of four-year college faculty when measured by the number of faculty who hold advanced degrees. Over three-fourths (81 percent) of all full time instructional faculty at public community colleges have at most the Master's degree. Well over half (68.1%) of the faculty of four-year colleges as compared to 16 percent of the faculty of two-year colleges have the Doctor of Philosophy (Ph.D.) degree. Almost twice as many faculty members are associate or full professors at four-year colleges (61.2%) than at two-year colleges (32%). Over a third (40%) of community college faculty hold the rank of instructor compared to 9% at four year colleges.[14] Even more (76%) part time community college faculty are at the rank of instructor. These are typically year to year appointments, thus, the stability of the faculty at the community college is at a higher turnover risk compared to faculty at four-year institutions.

In the future, differences may become even more pronounced between the faculty of community and four-year colleges. The division in graduate education between the Doctor of Arts (D.A.) degree and the Doctor of Philosophy (Ph.D.) degree is growing. The need for community college faculty to hold the traditional, research-oriented Ph.D., degree is being questioned by community college administrators and teachers.[15] The Carnegie Commission supports this division of graduate education. The D.A. is not a research-oriented degree and is viewed as more appropriate for community college instructors. Community colleges emphasize classroom teaching not the scholarly advancement of a discipline. Thus, over half (58.2%) of all faculty at community colleges teach 15 or more hours per week. Fewer (17.9%) faculty at four-year institutions teach as much--even few faculty (13.6%) at public doctoral institutions teach 15 or more hours per week.[16]

THE IMPORTANCE OF TYPE OF EDUCATIONAL EXPERIENCE

Many researchers have analyzed the relationship between educational experience and labor market outcomes. Generally this research shows that the number of years of education an individual acquires is a significant determinant of income and occupational status when social background is held constant. It is well known that acquiring four years of a college education and acquisition of the bachelor's degree enhances both adult earning ability and occupational status attainment.[17] Studies have shown, though, that having part of a four-year college education is of limited socioeconomic value.[18] Given the growth in the number of community colleges, and the growth in enrollment at these colleges, the need exists for analyses that distinguish socioeconomic rates of return to education not only by years of schooling attained but also by type of college entered. It does not make sense, nor does it portray the reality of higher education today, to lump all students with one to three years of a higher education together. Different kinds of educational institutions exist. To put all those who have less than four years of college into one group neglects the complex reality of higher education today.

Jerome Karabel's early work shows individuals from lower socioeconomic backgrounds are more likely to attend community colleges than are others. Community college students come from lower social class backgrounds as measured by parental income, occupational status, and education than four-year college entrants.[19] Nineteen consecutive surveys of college freshmen, by the American Council of Education, have shown that the social composition of the community college population is lower than at four-year institutions. In the mid-1980s, the proportion of students from families with incomes less than $25,000 at community colleges, four-year colleges, and universities was 48.3 percent, 39.9 percent, and 28.7 percent respectively.[20] Two-year colleges function as gates of entry into the higher educational system for large numbers of less economically advantaged students as well as for women and minority students. It is well known that community college entrants tend to be drawn from less advantaged socioeconomic backgrounds than four-year entrants. Entering a community college may well be perceived, by both parents and students coming from a less advantaged socioeconomic position than others, as an appropriate college choice. For students coming from lower parental socioeconomic backgrounds, the idea of acquiring the four-year college bachelor's degree may be one mixed with conflict. The lower the socioeconomic ranking, the less education one's father, mother, and oldest older sibling have generally acquired. How type of first college entered impacts years of schooling acquired, independent of other variables especially parental socioeconomic status, is critically important to the understanding of any status attainment model.

THE BACCALAUREATE ATTAINMENT GAP

Some see the community college as a place where students can demonstrate to others that they are four-year college material. The assumption underlying this view is that the two playing fields are fair and equal. In reality, community college entrants must prove themselves in a way that is not true for four-year college entrants. Community college entrance, in itself, presents a barrier to degree completion for community college entrants that is lacking in a four-year college environment. Community college transfer students' success in finishing the bachelor's degree is sharply lower than those who first enter a four-year college.

Early work found a baccalaureate attainment gap of 20-22 percent between four-year college entrants and community college transfer students four years after college entrance. Later work by Valez, who tracked the progress of the high school class of 1972, found a 48 percent baccalaureate attainment gap between four-year entrants and community college transfer students seven years after college entrance.[21] This gap continues to hold. In 1989-90, 57 percent of first time beginning students seeking a bachelor's degree who began at a four-year institution had completed the degree five years later, compared to 8 percent of comparable students who began at a community college.[22]

Dougherty suggests that the increase in the baccalaureate attainment gap between the 1960s and the 1980s is a reflection, in part, of the changed community college mission. He argues that today's community college student is less apt to receive rigorous academic preparation or encouragement to further their higher education. On the other hand, some maintain that community college students who are successful at transferring to a four-year school represent an elite group within the community college population. These students may have as good a chance as anyone to achieve academic success.[23] Notably, by 1997, work published by the United States Department of Education states that "although attending a community college may make good financial sense, it may not be conducive to completing a bachelor's degree."[24]

Community college students who want to acquire the bachelor's degree must successfully transfer. On entering a four-year institution they may still need to complete part of a general education curriculum in order to fulfill current institutional requirements for graduation. Further, some courses, especially "upper division" courses in the major, may transfer in as hours but not as a specific course. In other words, if a student takes a 200 level Marriage and Family class at the community college, the same class is likely to be listed as a 300 level class at the university. Most four-year institutions will not accept this class as an upper division elective. This, I believe, is largely because four-year institutions are protecting their programs and because there is a perception that the quality of instruction at the community college leaves something to be desired. The end result is that students may experience frustration with the transfer process and may be discouraged at how many additional hours they must complete to finish the bachelor's degree.

Recently, some institutions are entering into two by two agreement programs. Within a given state, a community college and a particular four year institution will link up. Essentially if a community college student completes a transfer oriented associate's degree, then general education requirements at the four year institution will be waived. There may still be a few additional college requirements, besides major requirements, nevertheless, the transfer process should be smoother and more advantageous to the student than the process of reviewing each class to make a determination regarding transfer status. Next, I turn to look at competing paradigms that aim to explain the role of higher education in our society. First, the functional interpretation of educational experience will be examined. Human capital theory, which in many ways supports functional theory, will also be reviewed. Finally, conflict theory will be explored in an effort to better understand the role of community colleges in the higher educational system.

Functional and Conflict Theories of Educational

Experience and Labor Market Outcomes

It is well-known that educational attainment shapes adult socioeconomic status. The importance of education, therefore, occupies a central place in both sociology and economics. Sociologists examine education primarily in relation to stratification and mobility. Economists analyze the rate of return to different educational outcomes and the relation between productivity and educational attainment. While the concerns of both disciplines differ, it would be a mistake to treat the knowledge gained in the study of each as a separate concern. This would thwart the advancement of our understanding of both educational experience and labor markets. In this chapter, I examine insights from functional and conflict theories in order to better understand differences in educational experience and labor market outcomes.

Functionalism emphasizes ability and choice in educational and career success. Functionalists presume that many options are open to individuals and that they consciously choose the option that is most beneficial. On the other hand, conflict theory rests on the idea that social class background and differentiation of higher education into sectors are important factors shaping an individual's educational attainment and adult socioeconomic status. Conflict theorists emphasize that various groups in society have different interests. Groups with power enjoy an advantage in society as their interests are those that are met.

A FUNCTIONAL THEORY OF EDUCATIONAL
EXPERIENCE AND LABOR MARKET OUTCOMES

In his book, *Social Theory and Social Structure* (1949), Robert Merton explores the different ways in which the word function has been used. Merton writes that the term has its most precise meaning when it refers to a variable considered in relation to other variables, in terms of which it may be expressed, or on the value of which its own value depends. Sociologists use the term function in a related less precise way in terms like functional interdependence and functional relations. Merton argues that the mathematical sense of the term function coupled with the notion of reciprocal relation is central to understanding the meaning of functional analysis in sociology.[1] Functionalists do not emphasize historical origins of the object in their analyzes. They tend to look at the objective consequences or the functions of a patterned and repetitive item which makes for the adaptation or adjustment of the system.

According to van den Berghe, the basic postulates of functionalism are: societies must be looked at holistically as systems of integrated parts; causation is multiple and reciprocal; social systems are fundamentally in a state of dynamic equilibrium; dysfunctions tend to resolve themselves or become institutionalized; changes occur in gradual adjustive patterns; change comes from adjustments to extra-systemic change, growth or inventions within society; and finally there exists a consensus on values.[2] Functionalists see much sharing of values and beliefs within a society. The social system is perceived as a complex interdependent one. Given this understanding, it is not surprising that functionalists believe social change must come very gradually as other system parts must be given the chance to adjust so that a general social equilibrium may be maintained. Functionalists see the social system as basically fair where all have to opportunity to succeed.

Alvin Gouldner, in *The Coming Crisis of Western Sociology* (1970), writes that Western sociology was a response to a utilitarian culture. He examines utilitarian culture and the middle class that he sees as Western sociology's historical bearer. With the rise of the middle class in the eighteenth century, utility emerged as a dominant social standard. Adults and adult roles became increasingly judged in terms of the usefulness imputed to them. Utilitarianism was linked to universalism because the value of utility was applied to all. At the same time, Gouldner suggests that utilitarianism depersonalized the individual by conceiving of them in terms only of utility. Utility and function grew into a way of talking about the usefulness of all social relations, behaviors, and beliefs. How was the existence of anything understood unless it was thought to be of some utility. These ideas certainly held in regard to a functionalist understanding of the educational institution.

In a society that emphasizes achievement, the educational system functions as a filtering mechanism for placing people in different occupational positions according to ability. The school is a place where all individuals can prove their worth. Rewards go to those who undertake the training necessary to enter positions deemed important by the society as a whole. Taking a functional perspective, those positions that offer the highest rewards are those that are of the greatest importance to the society and usually require the greatest training and talent. The classic example of this case is that of medical doctors. The presumption was that individuals would not acquire the education necessary to enter this position, given the difficulty and expense of the training, unless the prospect of a large future reward was in the picture. Interestingly, financial rewards, in this model, are assumed to be the critical motivating reward. Little exploration was given to the idea that individuals might be motivated by non-pecuniary considerations.

Functionalism in educational research in the 1950s was marked by a concern for the preservation of human resources. Technological functionalism in education focused on selection, training, and connections between the educational system and other major institutions.[3] Education came to be seen as a way to increase the efficiency of industrial society by the proper selection and channeling of human resources. This argument helped to support the rise of vocational guidance and the grouping of students according to their ability as determined by an IQ type test. Tracking and guidance became an increasingly important part of the process of getting into college, the kind of college attended, and the curriculum pursued. Certainly, by high school, students have experienced the impact of tracking in the educational system.

Today, forms of tracking exist at all school levels. Proponents of tracking believe students benefit as teachers can better address student needs. Less school time must be devoted to review and more material may be covered. Critics are concerned that tracking produces a type of self fulfilling prophesy. If students are tracked in less fast paced classes, they may assume a negative label as regards their academic talent. If little is expected from them, they may well produce less. Further, instructors might have a bias to see less in their work than in a system where tracking was not present. Technological functionalism supported the idea of equality of opportunity because all individuals should be given a chance to succeed. This helped to justify educational expansion and differentiation in the post-war period.[4]

From a functionalist view, education was viewed as benefitting both the economy and the individual. In his book, *The Economic Value of Education* (1963), Theodore Schultz sees the economy gaining from educational research, the discovery of talent, the cultivation of talent and the preparation of teachers. The individual's investment in education also includes their ability to earn a higher income as they attain more education. Education provides individuals with a greater range of job opportunities. Schultz also argues that leisure time is enhanced as educational attainment rises.

HUMAN CAPITAL THEORY

The expansion of educational institutions and enrollment during the post-war period gave rise to the question of the worth of education. What were its real costs and benefits? Human capital theory helped to justify educational growth by interpreting the process of acquiring skills through education as a matter of productive investment.[5] Human capital theory lends support to the democratization of access to education since economists see investment in education and socioeconomic returns to education as significantly linked. Since human resources should not be wasted, everyone should be given the opportunity to try. Karabel and Halsey observe that both human capital theory and functionalism stress the technical function of education and emphasize the efficient use of human resources.[6]

Human capital theory views education as a form of investment and consumption. Education has traditionally been seen as a form of consumption because it is a positive experience--especially when compared to alternatives to attending school. By emphasizing its economic value, education is no longer justifiable as a luxury for the few. The economic consequences of having an education are too significant. This focuses attention on equality of educational opportunity in a society that emphasizes the democratic nature of its opportunity structure.

Given a human capital perspective, individuals invest in education and one assumes that these individuals are more productive than others with less education. Therefore, they must be financially compensated. Kingsley Davis and Wilbert Moore argue this point in the case of medical doctors. They suggest that since a medical education is so burdensome a reward is necessary to compensate the investment, namely the prospect of a high future income. Otherwise, they argue, few if any students would become doctors.[7] This view is consistent with marginal productivity theory which states that wages are determined according to the worker's marginal contribution to the revenues of the firm. In a competitive market, more productive workers should be paid more all else equal.

In education, much research has been done that utilizes a human capital framework. In economics, human capital theory is the dominant theoretical explanation of the relation between earnings and education. Many studies show a correlation between education and income. Beyond stating that such a relation exists, most researchers are interested in analyzing the rate of return to the educational investment.

When analyzing returns to education, the assumption stands that there are measurable returns to the individual and to the society. Such returns are usually analyzed in terms of income as this is easily measured. Sociologists and economists analyze rates of return associated with each additional year of schooling. Some researchers are analyzing how educational quality (as measured by per pupil expenditures) fits into the human capital model.[8] Early research in this area, though, ignored how rates of return to education varied by type of college entered. In other words, are educational attainment differences shaped by whether or not a student first enters a community or a four-year college all else equal.

One of the most important works in education which utilizes a human capital framework is Gary Becker's *Human Capital* (1964). In this book, Becker argues that earnings vary over an individual's life-cycle according to a typical age-earning profile. He maintains that educational level affects the height of the age-earning profile. Richard Freeman outlines an age-earning profile in his book, *The Overeducated American* (1976). College students between the ages 18-22 earn less money than high school graduates who enter the labor force immediately after graduation. After the age of 22, income differences between the two groups diverge. For people who go to college, peak-earning ability is around age 57, later than the peak-earning period for high school graduates.[9] Human capital theorists suggest this is because returns on an educational investment continue to be of value as a person gets older, whereas returns from physical labor diminish with the passage of time.

Elchanan Cohn derives income differentials from Freeman's age-earning profile in his book *The Economics of Education* (1979). He defines the breakeven point, the age where income between those with just a high school certificate and college graduates are roughly equal, as age 25. After age 25, income differentials increase as college educated people reap the benefit of their educational choice. In estimating lifetime income differentials between white male high school graduates who did not

go to college and white male college graduates, Cohn finds that the college graduates
earn $582,576 (in 1997 constant dollars) more during their lifetime than the high
school graduates.

Much criticism has been leveled at human capital theory. Some economists
argue that credentialism may be the important link between education and earnings.[10]
Michael Spence suggests that the credential, or the degree, is a signal to employers
that an individual has certain attributes. Attributes that the individual had before they
entered college; attributes which employers believe produce good workers. The
degree merely certifies the presence of such attributes. Credentialism, Medina
argues, is based on conflict theory. Basically, those with the resources to do so enter
prestigious colleges which signals potential employers where they are
socioeconomically situated in the social order.[11] Porter goes on to suggest that
credentialism is a new form of stratifiction involving the right to work. In other
words, if one does not have the "right" credential their ability to support themselves
is on shakier ground.[12] Human capital and functional theory rest on a consensus or
integration model of society. Implicit in these frameworks is the idea that schooling
in the United States is meritocratic. In a meritocracy, individuals are assumed to
have free will. Individuals can attain as much education as they have the motivation
and ability to achieve. Responsibility for failure to succeed rests with the individual
as they did not take advantage of the means of success that were available.

Human capital theory views an individual's investment in self as a conscious
decision. The decision maker decides between the many options of investment that
are available and rationally chooses those investments that will most likely have the
greatest future pecuniary and nonpecuniary benefits. Human capital theory rests
heavily on the idea that individuals possess a future time orientation, an ability to
sacrifice goods today for more returns tomorrow. In other words, they have an ability
to defer gratification. What is lacking in human capital theory is a recognition that
individuals with a present time orientation do not choose instant gratification instead
of, for instance, investment in education. As Elliot Liebow writes, what appears as

a present time orientation to outsiders is, to the person experiencing it, as much a future time orientation as that of a middle class person. The real difference between the two does not lie in their different orientations to time, but in their different orientations to future time or, more specifically, to their different futures.[13]

The functional theory of educational experience and labor market outcomes outlined here can be viewed within a framework which emphasizes ability, skill, and investment in education. A functionalist would argue that community colleges provide all individuals an opportunity to enter the higher educational system. After getting a start at the community college, students may transfer to earn the bachelor's degree. From a functionalist view, beginning one's higher education at a community college rather than a four-year college would not have a deleterious impact on educational attainment or adult socioeconomic status. In other words, educational systems can be different but equal.

A CONFLICT THEORY OF EDUCATIONAL EXPERIENCE AND LABOR MARKET OUTCOMES

During the 1960s, the functionalist paradigm in sociology came increasingly under attack. In his book, *A Sociology of Sociology* (1970), Friedrichs outlines the paradigmatic revolution of this period. System and its attendant notion, functionalism, represented sociological orthodoxy in the 1950s. Daniel Bell's book *The End of Ideology* (1960) typifies this period of ideological detente. However, the end of ideology thesis, Friedrichs observes, became quite dated with the revolutionary events of the 1960s. Sociology entered a time of troubles. Thomas Kuhn views a period of crisis as a necessary prologue to the emergence of a new paradigm.[14] Systems theory could not account for fundamental social change. Functionalism was attacked as providing justification for the conservatism of the post-war period. The search for an alternative paradigm was on.

Alvin Gouldner begins *The Coming Crisis of Western Sociology* (1970) with the statement that social theorists were working within a crumbling social matrix--within the sound of guns. In *Coming Crisis*, he presents a critical analysis of the sociology of sociology concentrating on structural-functionalism as developed by Talcott Parsons. Assuming an ideological position which he believes contradicts the functional school, Gouldner argues that the sociologist is not a value-free creature but develops theory and research which is necessarily conditioned by personal beliefs and values.

Social theories, Gouldner writes, contain at least two elements. First are open theoretical assumptions. The second is a set of assumptions that are unpostulated or background assumptions. Some theories are intuitively convincing because they confirm an individual's background assumptions. Domain assumptions are background assumptions of more limited application about society. The work of sociologists, as well as others, is influenced by a sub-theoretical set of beliefs. The lifelong process of learning background assumptions begins while learning one's first language. Thus, the theorists must grasp two things. First, one must recognize that what is at issue is what is in the world and in oneself. Second, the theorist must have the courage of their convictions. Courage, at least, to acknowledge one's beliefs as their own whether or not they are legitimated by reason and evidence. Thus, every social theory is a personal theory rooted in a limited personal reality. Every social theory encourages us to change or to accept the world. Every social theory is a discreet obituary or celebration for a social order.[15]

Conflict theory emphasizes tension rather than equilibrium and conflict rather than integration. It is a perspective which stresses the significance of interests and power in social life.[16] Sociologists are not perceived as value-free creatures. Instead, as C. Wright Mills urged, sociologists should seek to understand the historical and social period of which they are a part in order to use their imaginations to unravel its dynamics of power and privilege. The task of understanding and perhaps changing our society became the focus of the sociological discipline in the 1960s. Conflict theory gave rise to many questions that could not be adequately examined within a functional perspective. More and more sociologists came to accept conflict theory as the predominant sociological theory of the age.

Human capital theory emerged in the 1960s at approximately the same time as conflict theory. However, human capital theory does not focus on problems of power or conflict. The different directions these two schools of thought took stems, in part, from different methodologies.

Economics today rests heavily on sophisticated mathematical proofs and techniques. Mathematical technique is the fundamental content of what is taught in graduate economic departments in the United States today. In their book, *The Market for Labor: An Analytical Treatment* (1979), John Addison and W. Stanley Siebert suggest that economics is best regarded as a technique for analyzing social problems rather than as a science in its own right.[17] Given such a sophisticated methodology, a methodology that takes many years to master, little attack can be lodged against the method by outsiders or even economists who have not had the training that is considered to represent orthodox economics today. The suggestion can be made that the discipline does not adequately deal with problems of power and conflict. However, critics with such concerns are on the fringe of the economics establishment. There is a consensus among economists that methodological empiricism represents the best way to examine economic reality.

The sociological discpline combines a mix of theory and mathematical methods. Much controversy surrounds methodological empiricism in sociological research and how methodology relates to theory. Further, there has been a resurgence of interest in historical/comparative sociology, phenomenology, ethnomethodology, critical sociology, and feminist thought.[18] The essential difference between economics and sociology is that sociologists seek to understand and explain social reality and social change. Economists, on the other hand, mathematically model that phase of human behavior which is related to the allocation of resources in the production and distribution of economic goods for the satisfaction of material desires. Mathematical technique is not at the heart of sociological analysis. The separation of higher education into sectors brings into question problems of conflict and social class. The fact that minorities, women, and those from working class backgrounds disproportionately attend community colleges cannot be dismissed as a matter of random circumstance. Human capital theory may be able to analyze economic differences by quality of institution attended, thereby picking up some differences by type of education; however, to analyze why different kinds of educational institutions exist and what the socioeconomic ramifications of their existence are for students is a difficult question for human capital theorists to unravel.

The reason conflict theorists emphasize the minority and economically disadvantaged student composition of the community college population is because of the link they see between type of first college entered and educational outcomes.[19] Conflict theorists argue that what type of college an individual enters affects how many years of schooling they attain and what kind of degree, if any, received. Of the two-thirds of community college entrants who want to transfer to a four-year college only one-third actually transfer.[20] Karabel argues that the likelihood of a student persisting in higher education is negatively influenced by attending a community college. Only 15-30 percent of community college entrants eventually graduate from a four-year college. On the other hand, 60-70 percent of students at large state universities graduate.[21] Conflict theorists believe that as long as the community college remains an institution where only a part of the college community vie for success while a more privileged sector sits in elite four-year institutions, the community college will remain an institution plagued by controversy in a society which stresses the democratic character of its opportunity structure.

Many see equal access to education as being at the core of the democratic struggle. The idea that there exists and open contest for mobility helps legitimate individual success and failure. Early studies analyzing the relationship between social class background, educational experience, and labor market outcomes showed social class as a major determinant of the length, quality, and type of education individuals experience.[22] This view has gradually been supplanted by one which emphasizes the importance of an independent effect of education on socioeconomic status.[23] This leads to the view that education is a way to overcome the influence of social class background on career opportunities.

SOCIAL SORTING FUNCTION OF THE COMMUNITY COLLEGE

How the community college performs its role as a social-sorting institution and how this function is perceived is very important in whether or not the educational system is viewed as legitimate. In *The Open-Door College* (1960), Burton Clark describes the community college as a place where many students reach undesired destinations. Most community college students enter with the hope of transferring to a four-year college. Those students who are perceived as having the ability to transfer and those who enter the community college for vocational study are not problematic. Problems arise for students who want to transfer yet are not perceived by others as having the ability to do so. These students are cooled out in the community college.[24] Faced with tests, counselors, administrators, these latent-terminal community college students come to see their first choice as perhaps not so appropriate. These students drop out or go into a vocational field. They view this as an appropriate change not as a failure.

The dilemma of the role of the community college, Clark argues, is that the cooling-out function needs to remain reasonably latent. In other words, the process must not be clearly perceived or understood by prospective students. Should this function become obvious, then the ability of the community college to perform it would be impaired. It would turn the pressure for college admission back on four-year colleges. The overt determination of what kind of educational opportunity an individual deserves cannot be made within the context of an open contest for mobility. The use of IQ tests to objectively determine an individual's ability to learn, where such tests help sort individuals into different kinds of schools, different tracks, and differentiated subject matter, is questionable within the context of a democracy.

What could be more undemocratic than to track low IQ students, many times from working-class backgrounds, into vocational programs because a determination was made that they could not be educated?[25]

In analyzing how ability and social class background shape socioeconomic attainment one must quantify each in order to determine its relative significance. In the literature, ability is commonly defined as those biological, psychological, and internalized cultural factors that determine an individual's capacity to succeed. Ability is usually operationalized by taking an individual's score on an IQ-type test.

EDUCATIONAL ATTAINMENT AND SOCIAL CLASS BACKGROUND

One definition of social class background refers to the class to which an individual belongs in relation to the mode of production. In the Marxian tradition, class is a social relation, a relationship-in-process.[26] This concept is difficult to quantify adequately. Thus, contemporary sociologists analyze stratification within a society and define positions in the stratified order (socioeconomic background) in accordance with a set of indices. Most researchers define an individual's socioeconomic class background as a composite of their father's and mother's educational attainment, father's occupational status and family income. Socioeconomic status is defined in this way because it is widely accepted and because the data researchers utilize makes it difficult to define socioeconomic background in any other way. Once defined, background variables must be held constant in analyzing school effects on socioeconomic status. In this way, one can analyze if educational attainment, ability, and parental socioeconomic status independently shape earning ability and occupational status.

Much evidence can be cited which suggests that the quality of college one attends does not modify prior socioeconomic background differences.[27] Sewell and Hauser argue that differences in labor market experiences due to college education can best be understood by recognizing the nonrandom allocation of students to different types of colleges. They see selection and recruitment criteria as the real factors in the relationship between college differences and socioeconomic achievements. They argue that ability, socioeconomic status, and a student's college goal must be held constant in analyzing returns to education, otherwise, they believe, their effects may wrongly be attributed to the effect of college differences.

Other researchers find significant socioeconomic differences between groups by the type and quality of college attended.[28] They maintain that type of first college entered is important in determining educational attainment and adult socioeconomic status. Social class background is important in what kind of college an individual enters. Further, type of first college entered significantly affects a student's educational attainment and adult socioeconomic status independent of social class background or years of education. Type of first college entered shapes our life chances.

EDUCATIONAL ATTAINMENT AND ABILITY

Most researchers recognize that ability is an important factor in analyzing type of first college entered and adult socioeconomic status differences. They differ in how they perceive ability, opportunity, and the significance of ability in the educational process. Samuel Bowles and Herbert Gintis argue that IQ, while important to educational and economic success, derives its significance from the common association between social class background and level of schooling. They suggest that, for the vast majority of people, intellectual abilities developed or certified in school may contribute little to getting ahead. The fact that success tends to run in families arises virtually independently from any genetic inheritance of IQ. IQ, they contend, is not an important intrinsic criterion for economic success. Rather IQ-ism hides the importance of social class background in educational attainment and career opportunities and lends support to the notion that American education is meritocratic.[29]

Madan Sarup also questions the validity of IQ tests. Taking a phenomenological position, Sarup argues that individuals should not be categorized by the use of such tests. Sarup maintains that cognition is related to cultural context and that differences in IQ between racial groups, for instance, may be related to style of thinking rather than innate ability.[30] Tracking, by the use of IQ tests, is self-validating in that it manufactures the differences which justify its existence. It is through processes such as these that success is guaranteed for some whereas there is the institutionalization of failure for others. Proponents of community colleges stress their role in democratizing higher education largely by providing an equal opportunity to enter the higher educational system. On the other hand, one could argue, in light of the above critique, that community colleges may be structurally reproducing a class-based tracking system into United States higher education.

RESEARCH QUESTIONS EXAMINED

Since a comprehensive theory of the relationship between educational experience and labor markets has yet to be formulated, questions informed by functionalism, human capital theory and conflict theory are examined. The basic questions explored in this work are:

(1) What factors shape community college compared to four-year college entrance? How does community college entrance shape the likelihood of acquiring the Bachelor's degree? Is the social-sorting function of schools legitimate in that those students who are most able will succeed? How does type of first college entered shape the likelihood of achieving one's educational goals?

(2) Do schools modify the consequences of social class background differences so that ability is an important variable in career achievement regardless of type of first college entered? What variables are important in understanding differences in adult socioeconomic status?

Next I turn to an examination of the first question, namely what factors are important in shaping the probability of community college versus four-year college entrance and acquisition of the bachelor's degree. For further information on the methodology used in conducting the research in order to delve into these questions, see Appendix A at the end of the text.

Who Enters Community and Four-Year Colleges?
Who Aquires the Bachelor's Degree?

Who Enters Community and Four-Year Colleges?

Who Acquires the Bachelor's Degree?

This chapter analyzes factors that shape the likelihood of community college entrance compared to four-year college entrance with background variables constant. In other words, what factors are important in understanding where one enters the higher educational system after taking into account differences in socioeconomic status, IQ, and other background variables. Are some groups more likely than others to begin their higher education at the community college versus a four year college or university? In addition, I examine the effect of region (south/not in the south) in shaping the likelihood of entering a community college versus a four-year institution. Community colleges are more prevalent outside of the South, thus students residing outside of the South should be more likely to enter community colleges than four-year institutions because there are more community college institutions in the area. Those that live in the South may have more variety in type of institution in which to enrol. In this work, Southern states include: Delaware, Maryland, the District of Columbia, Virginia, West Virginia, North Carolina, South Carolina, Georgia, Florida, Kentucky, Tennessee, Alabama, Mississippi, Arkansas, Louisiana, Oklahoma, and Texas. All other states would be considered out of the south.

In their work, Alexander, Holupa and Pallas find that the probability of four-year college entrance is higher for blacks than others.[1] In other words, an African American college student is more apt to enter a four year college rather than a community college. Their work fails, however, to control for the effect of region. Given the small number of traditionally black four-year colleges outside of the South, I will also look at a possible interaction between the variables race and region. This allows me to examine differences in likelihood of community college entrance for blacks compared to whites living outside the South.

I expect that African Americans will be more apt to enter community colleges outside the South because relatively high numbers of black college entrants, especially those in the South, will enter historically black four-year colleges. For example, *half* of all African American four-year public college students in the state of Virginia attend Norfolk State University or Virginia State University. In a state where higher education was historically segregated, these are the two public four-year institutions in the state geared toward serving African American students.[2]

There is evidence that going to a college or university is still perceived by both parents and students as more appropriate for men than women.[3] We know little, though, about the likelihood of entering college, especially a community or four-year college, and how this varies by gender and measured ability. Therefore, I will also look at the interaction between the variables gender and IQ. I expect that women, even women who perform well on IQ type tests, will be more likely to enter a community college than a four-year institution compared to comparable men. Entering a community college may well be perceived as a more "appropriate" college choice for women than for men.

BACHELOR'S DEGREE COMPLETION

After analyzing varying probabilities of community college versus four-year college entrance, I turn to examine the likelihood of achieving the bachelor's degree. The critical variable I examine is whether or not type of first college entered is a significant variable in shaping the likelihood of achieving the bachelor's degree. In other words, does it make a difference in likelihood of bachelor degree completion whether or not a person starts their higher education at a community college rather than a four-year institution? My work recognizes that students begin their higher education at different type of colleges. Thus, this work sheds lights on how differentiation in the structure of United States higher education shapes the educational attainment process. The complexities of how the division of higher education into a two tiered system shapes the status attainment process is an area that merits further research attention.

I expect that type of first college entered college independently shape the odds of bachelor's degree completion. In other words, if one aims to achieve the bachelor's degree, it makes a difference where they begin their higher education. Specifically, the likelihood of completing the four year bachelor's degree varies between community college and four year college entrants even after background differences have been taken into account.

If this is the case, mine is a conservative test of a link between type of college entered and bachelor degree success. This is because I do not restrict the definition of degree success by a particular time period, for example, four or six years. Rather if a person completed the bachelor's degree, regardless of how long it may have taken to do so, they are included in my analysis. In future research, it would be revealing to analyze how type of first college entered shapes the likelihood of completion of the bachelor's degree within a four, five, and six year time frame. The four, five, and six year time frames are the traditional length of time taken to complete the bachelor's degree. If anything, colleges and universities today aim to streamline curricula to ensure that students may complete the bachelor's degree in four years of full time work.

In their work, Alba and Lavin found that students who entered a four year college in the City University of New York system (CUNY) had a distinct advantage in likelihood of bachelor's degree completion compared to comparable CUNY community college students.[4] Using regression analysis, they found community college entrance had a modest negative effect on successfully completing one's educational aspirations net of background variables. In other words, they found that, in terms of how far one wants to go in the educational system, it makes a difference where one begins their higher education. Specifically, if one begins their higher education at a community college, they do not have the same chance to finish their desired educational work as does a four-year college entrant. This effect holds when differences in ability, gender, race, and other background variables are taken in account. I expect that Alba and Lavin's general results will be replicated in this work.

What is lacking in the current literature is an understanding of WHY community college entrants are less likely to complete the bachelor's degree than four-year entrants all else equal. It is well known that community college entrants tend to be drawn from less advantaged socioeconomic backgrounds than four-year entrants. Entering a community college may well be perceived, by both parents and students coming from a less advantaged socioeconomic position than others, as an appropriate college choice. The lower the socioeconomic ranking, the less education the individuals' father, mother, and oldest older sibling acquired. For students coming from lower parental socioeconomic backgrounds, the idea of acquiring the four-year college bachelor's degree may be one mixed with conflict. By acquiring more education, they will be quite different, in terms of educational experience, from others in their family of origin. Thus, an independent association between parental socioeconomic background and acquisition of the bachelor's degree bodes ill for a community college entrant's degree success as a disproportionate number of community college entrants are drawn from lower socioeconomic backgrounds. In a way, community colleges may reinforce socioeconomic divisions within the society as a whole.

Some see the community college as a place where students can demonstrate to others that they are college material. If one did not perform well academically in high school, then the community college offers the opportunity to change course. A problem with this view is an assumption that the two playing fields are fair and equal. To explore this idea, an interaction between the variables IQ and type of first college entered will be explored in regard to bachelor's degree completion. I expect that IQ will be more important in shaping the likelihood of bachelor's degree completion for community college than four-year college entrants. I believe that community college entrants must prove themselves in a way that does not hold true for four year entrants. This finding would suggest an institutional dimension exists in shaping differences in bachelor degree completion rates between two-year and four-year entrants.

To add empirical support to the idea that an institutional effect exists in shaping bachelor degree completion between community and four-year college entrants, another interaction term will be examined. I will look at an interaction between the variables goal and type of first college entered. I expect that it will be less likely that a community college entrant, who wants to finish the bachelor's degree, acquires the degree than a comparable four-year entrant. Two year and four year institutions are vastly different kinds of institutions. Community college entrance, in itself, by the very nature of the community college institution, presents a formidable barrier to bachelor degree completion for community college entrants that is lacking in a four-year college environment. Institutional barriers, in the community college system, that may help create this difference include guidance counseling and testing. Further, a self-selection process in undoubtedly at work. Students who feel less secure about entering the higher educational system, may disproportionately select community college over four year college entrance. If faced with a barrier in the community college environment, they may be more apt to drop out or to pursue a vocational education. This is basically the process Burton Clark termed the cooling out effect which was discussed earlier in this work. On the average, perhaps community college students never had the confidence in their own ability as did four year college entrants. Self-selection, lack of institutional support to transfer, and the transfer process itself must be considered in understanding why bachelor degree completion rates for community college entrants lag behind those of comparable four year college entrants.

ANALYZING THE DATA

As expected, students coming from a less advantaged parental socioeconomic background and those who score lower on tests of mental ability have higher odds of entering a community college than a four-year institution. Alternatively, students who come from higher parental socioeconomic backgrounds and those who score higher on IQ type tests are more likely than others to enter four year colleges rather than community colleges. Not surprisingly, students who do not have the bachelor's degree as a goal are more likely to enter a community college than a four-year institution.

As hypothesized, living outside the South is positively associated with community college entrance. If you live outside of the South then the odds are higher that you will go to a community college not a four year institution, all else equal. Also, as hypothesized African American students who live outside the South are significantly more likely to enter a community college versus a four year college than are comparable whites. This finding lends support to the idea that African American students may well benefit from the existence of historically black public four year college in the South in a way that has not been recognized in past research. If community college entrance has a negative impact on bachelor degree completion, compared with four year college entrance, and given that African Americans residing outside the South are more apt to enter community college not four year institutions in part because of the relative lack of historically black four year institutions in the region, part of what shapes differences in bachelor degree completion rates by race are consequences of differentiation in the structure of higher education.

The higher one scores on an IQ-type test the less likely they are to enter a community college. As expected, this relationship holds stronger for men than women. All else the same, a man who scores well on an IQ type test is more likely to enter a four-year college not a community college than is a comparable woman. This lends support to the idea that women who perform well on IQ tests are more likely to enter a community college than a four-year school versus comparable men. In other words, "being smart" does more to boost the odds of four-year college entrance for men, on average, than for women.

ACQUISITION OF THE BACHELOR'S DEGREE

As expected, four-year college entrance is positively associated with completion of the bachelor's degree. It is more likely that one will acquire the bachelor's degree if they first entered a four-year college rather than a community college all else equal. In other words, after taking other factors into account it makes a difference in likelihood of degree completion what kind of school a student enters. Community college entrants are not as likely as comparable four-year college entrants to finish the bachelor's degree. This finding is in line with advise now given in work published by the United States Department of Education. By 1997, officials at the Department of Education recognized that "although attending a community college may make good financial sense, it may not be conducive to completing a bachelor's degree."[5]

As hypothesized, students coming from advantaged parental socioeconomic backgrounds have higher odds of finishing the bachelor's degree. The more formal education an individual's parents and oldest sibling acquired boosts her/his odds of finishing the bachelor's degree all else equal. Since community college entrants tend to come from less advantaged parental socioeconomic backgrounds, this association does not bode well for their successfully completing the degree. Since the community college population is over-represented by students from poorer parental socioeconomic backgrounds, and given that community college entrants are less likely than others to finish the bachelor's degree all else equal, then the community college institution helps function to reproduce inequality within the society as a whole.

Besides four-year college entrance and coming from a higher socioeconomic background, having the bachelor's degree as a goal, being male, and having higher measured mental ability are also positively associated with acquisition of the bachelor's degree. Variation in race and region have virtually no independent effect on finishing the degree when controlling for other background variables. In other words, there is no statistically significant difference in degree completion between blacks and whites or those who live in the South compared to those who live out of the South after taking into account other differences.

As hypothesized, increased mental ability significantly bettered the odds of finishing the bachelor's degree for community college entrants more so than for four-year college entrants. Community colleges may be places where students must demonstrate their potential to do well in college. This is a hurdle that their four-year college peers do not have to jump. Four-year college entrants have a better chance to finish the degree regardless of how well they score on mental ability tests. It is assumed that four- year college entrants can do college level work. Community college entrants, on the other hand, have to pass the hurdle of demonstrating their ability in the community college population in their successful quest for the bachelor's degree. Thus, for those who do not perform well on IQ type tests, the decision to enter a community college rather than a four year college may be a risky one if one aims to finish the bachelor's degree.

As one would expect, the odds of finishing the bachelor's degree, if this is one's goal, are significantly higher if an individual first enters a four-year college rather than a community college. The odds of finishing the bachelor's degree for four-year college entrants, who have this as an educational goal, are more than three times higher than for comparable community college entrants. Community college entrance introduces a structural barrier for a student that they must get past to acquire the bachelor's degree. This is an institutional barrier that does not exist in the four-year college environment.

Since not all community college entrants want to acquire the bachelor's degree, I also analyzed the subset of the community college population who have the bachelor's degree as an educational goal. Once again, the odds of four- year college entrants eventually acquiring the bachelor's degree were higher than for community college entrants. The only variables that are more important than type of first college entered in understanding variation in degree completion odds are parental socioeconomic background and mental ability. What shapes this gap in bachelor degree completion rates between comparable community college and four year college entrants must be addressed in future research. Given the numbers of students who begin their higher education at a community college, it is in the interests of students, their families, and the society as a whole to better understand this difference in bachelor degree completion rates. This is a public policy issue that has been ignored for too long.

DISCUSSION

Compared to four-year college entrance, community college entrance is negatively associated with the likelihood of finishing the bachelor's degree all else equal. This, coupled with the fact that students coming from a less advantaged parental socioeconomic background are most likely to enter a community college not a four-year school, raises equality of opportunity questions. Entering a community college introduces a structural barrier to completion of the bachelor's degree. Regardless of ability, motivation to acquire the degree, gender, or race, the mere decision to begin one's higher education at a community college makes it less likely that a student will ever complete the degree. Channeling disproportionate numbers of students from low socioeconomic status backgrounds into community colleges guarantees a double negative status in their quest for a bachelor's degree. Even for community college entrants who want to acquire the degree and for those who score well on IQ tests, community college entrance has a deleterious effect on degree completion. We must delve into this question: Why do some students have to overcome structural barriers in their quest for a bachelor's degree that other students never face?

First College Entered, Occupational Status, and Gender

Given the increases in the number of and enrollment in community colleges, a need exists for analyzes that distinguish occupational status differences not only by years of schooling acquired but also by type of college entered. Lumping together all students with one to three years of a college education does not portray the reality of higher education today because different kinds of educational institutions exist. How structural differentiation of higher education affects occupational achievements of both women and men is an important, yet neglected, area of analysis.

In analyzing occupational differences by type of first college entered, I examine what function the community college system performs in our society. Are community colleges an extension of a class-based tracking system in higher education, or are they the avenues for upward mobility that their supporters claim?

Further, I look at how occupational status differences differ between men and women and how this is shaped by type of first college entered. Does the decision to enter a community college versus a four year institution impact occupational status attainment of women more so than for men. Do racial differences significantly shape occupational status attainment after variation in type of first college entered have been taken into account? These are some of the issues addressed here.

FIRST COLLEGE ENTERED, EDUCATIONAL ATTAINMENT, AND OCCUPATIONAL STATUS

Differences in educational outcomes, as well as class background, exist between community and four-year college entrants. The community college institution has generally been perceived as a transfer-oriented institution.[1] Most community college students want to transfer to a four-year college; however, few actually do. Only 24 percent of women and 25 percent of the men enrolled in two-year institutions transferred to four-year institutions.[2] Few community college entrants (21 percent) achieve the associate's degree. The associate's degree is the terminal degree offered by community colleges. The degree may be in a liberal arts or vocational field of study. Traditionally, four year institutions do not accept the vocational degree in the transfer process. In fact, there are often restrictions on what will transfer and what will not transfer when a student pursues a liberal arts curriculum.

Most community college entrants drop out of college.[3] The majority of students (60-70 percent) at large state universities, on the other hand, do graduate. What shapes the high drop out rate within the community college is a topic that has received sparse research attention. I believe it is critical to better understand the processes that shape retention rates within various types of institutions so that students and parents may make better informed decisions about the college choice.

DESCRIPTIVE ANALYSIS OF OCCUPATIONAL DIFFERENCES BETWEEN COMMUNITY COLLEGE AND FOUR YEAR COLLEGE ENTRANTS

The type of college an individual enters shapes adult occupational status. Occupations are here categorized into three major groups: professional and managerial workers, white-collar workers, and blue-collar workers. White collar workers include sales and clerical occupational categories. Blue collar workers would be employed as manual or production laborers. Among my sample, community college entrants are more than twice as likely to hold blue-collar jobs as are four-year college entrants. Almost twice as many four-year college entrants are in professional or managerial occupations as are community college entrants.

Highest degree received also shapes adult occupational status. More than three times as many associate of arts degree recipients as bachelor of arts recipients hold blue-collar jobs. Most associate degree recipients, in this sample, hold white-collar jobs, whereas most bachelor recipients are in professional or managerial positions. More than twice as many bachelor recipients as associate degree recipients hold professional jobs. Analyzing occupational differences for community college associate degree recipients, by field of degree, shows that more than twice as many associate degree recipients in vocational fields hold blue-collar jobs as do associate degree recipients in liberal arts fields. Entering a community college instead of a four-year college, obtaining an associate's degree rather than a bachelor's degree, and concentrating in a vocational, rather than liberal arts, field in acquiring the associate's degree, all entail a penalty in terms of adult occupational status. In other words, labor market employees with these backgrounds are more apt to be employed as blue-collar rather than white-collar or professional/managerial workers.

ANALYZING OCCUPATIONAL DIFFERENCES BY GENDER

In my sample, the mean number of years of education acquired by men and women is approximately the same. Further, there is less variance in the number of years of education women complete compared to the variance in the number of years of education completed by men. This findings supports the work of others who find that educational achievements of employed men and women are similar.[4]

The completion of an additional year of education is more important for men than women in shaping differences in occupational status. Men experience an increase in occupational prestige over their lifetime which is enhanced by completion of additional years of education. A woman's occupational status, on the other hand, tends to remain relatively constant throughout her lifetime.[5] Thus, regardless of her educational attainment, the occupational mobility a woman experiences in the labor market is less than the occupational mobility men experience. This is not to imply that educational achievements are unimportant for women. Rather, as regards occupational mobility, educational achievements do not yield a like return for women, as a group, as they do, on average, for men.

ANALYZING THE DATA

The benefit, in terms of adult occupational status, of entering a four-year college instead of a community college is greater for men than for women. Type of first college entered is a statistically significant variable in understanding differences in occupational status for all college entrants and for male college entrants, holding constant background variables. In other words, the mere act of beginning one's higher education at a community college rather than a four-year college is important in understanding differences in occupational status for all college students as well as specifically for men as a group.

This may indicate that men have a wider variety of career choices available to them than do women. Problems of occupational sex segregation mark the United States labor market. Women and men do not typically enter the same types of jobs. Even within a single occupational category, such as sales, there is gender segregation. For example, in sales it is well known that male workers tend to dominate high commission products within the sales field. Women, on the other hand, are overrepresented in less lucrative retail sales positions. Issues surrounding gender segregation of the labor market are at the crux of the comparable worth movement. Again, comparable worth advocates argue that jobs can be objectively evaluated, thereby, correcting labor market discrimination by gender.

Besides starting their higher education at a four-year school, men also benefit in terms of adult occupational status with additional years of work experience, being older, scoring higher on IQ type tests, completing additional years of education, acquiring the bachelor's degree, living in a metropolitan area, being white, and being married. The depressive effect of beginning higher education at a community college, rather than a four year college or university, persists regardless of subsequent educational history. Even with completion of the bachelor's degree, men who began their higher education at a community college remain at a disadvantage in regard to adult occupational status attainment compared to like four year college entrants.

OCCUPATIONAL RETURNS TO EDUCATION BY GENDER AND RACE

On average, additional years of education, or having the bachelor's degree, are worth more occupationally to women who enter four-year colleges than to women who enter community colleges. The completion of each additional year of education brings a higher occupational return to female four-year college entrants than female community college entrants. In other words, the pay off to finishing each additional year of education is greater for women who begin their higher education at a four-year institution than a community college, all else equal.

The benefit to finishing the bachelor's degree is also higher for female four-year college entrants than female community college entrants. Female four-year college entrants enjoy an occupational gain on finishing the bachelor's degree that female community college entrants who transfer to finish the four year degree never realize. The occupational pay off on the educational investment for female community college entrants comes with completion of each additional year of education, though less so than for female four-year college entrants, NOT on completion of the bachelor's degree.

Looking at differences between African American and white women, the data show that white women generally benefit more than African American women by *entering* a four-year college rather than a community college. However, African American women may benefit occupationally more than white women on completion of additional years of education. Since community college entrance has a deleterious effect on educational attainment, compared with four year college entrance, the benefit to African American women from beginning their higher education at a four-year college cannot be overlooked. Further, among four-year college entrants, white women who *completed* the bachelor's degree achieved, on average, relatively less occupationally than comparable African American women. Thus, African American women who first entered a four

year institution and who completed the bachelor's degree enjoyed more of an occupational benefit than did comparable white women.

African American women benefit occupationally on completion of the bachelor's degree regardless of type of first college entered. Future work needs to address the probability of achieving the bachelor's degree by type of first college entered, gender, and race. This may be a critical link for women, especially African American women, in how type of college entered shapes occupational returns to education. Thus, the evidence is mixed. Regardless of type of first college entered, African American women benefit occupationally from completing the bachelor's degree. African American women with the bachelor's degree benefit even more occupationally if they began their higher education at a four year college rather than a community college. This holds true for comparable white women as well.

THE EFFECTS OF TYPE OF FIRST COLLEGE ENTERED ON OCCUPATIONAL STATUS

Community college entrants, on the average, hold jobs that have a lower occupational status than four-year college entrants even after controlling for differences in years of education acquired and other background variables. Thus, a community college entrant with eighteen years of education will tend to hold a job with a lower occupational ranking than a comparable four-year college entrant. In other words, it makes a difference in understanding occupational status differences what type of college an individual enters as well as how many years of schooling they complete. In terms of adult occupational status, four-year college entrants gain more by completing each additional year of education than is true for community college entrants. Community college entrance negatively impacts occupational status compared to four-year college entrance. On the average, a community college entrant, who acquired the same number of years of education as a four year college entrant, will never realize the same occupational return on their educational investment. Further, if a student only acquires the associate's degree and does not go on to complete the bachelor's degree their occupational status is negatively impacted compared to a bachelor degree recipient. The associate's degree does not bring the same occupational rewards or returns as does a bachelor's degree. This information should be generally known as parents and students sort through choices in higher education in making the decision of what type of first college to enter and what type of degree to pursue.Community college entrants who acquire additional years of education enjoy higher occupational returns compared to community college entrants who acquire fewer years of education. Community college entrants with more years of education are more likely than others to transfer to a four-year college or university. This enhances the probability that they will achieve the bachelor's degree which in turn brings an occupational benefit to the community college entrant even if it is less of an occupational return than a comparable four year college entrant realizes.

Ability makes more of a difference in shaping adult occupational status for community college entrants than for four-year college entrants. One assumes that community college students who score high on IQ type tests are more likely to be in a college transfer track than community college entrants who score poorly on such tests. The effect of IQ is more important in the community college system because tracking is more evident in community colleges than in four-year colleges. Four-year college students are more likely to share a general liberal arts curriculum, regardless of ability, than are community college entrants. Thus, the function of tracking within the community college merits additional research attention as socioeconomic outcomes among community college entrants appear to be shaped by differences in measured ability.

Socioeconomic background makes more of a differences to four-year college entrants than community colleges entrants in shaping adult occupational status. A student from a high parental socioeconomic background is more likely to enter a four-year college than a community college. This, in turn, has an impact on both the number of years of education they attain and the kind of entry level position for which they qualify. Regardless of parental socioeconomic background, community college entrants have a lower occupational status than comparable four-year college entrants. This suggests that an institutional effect may exist in shaping an individual's educational achievements and adult occupational status. In other words, what kind of higher educational institution a student enters may shape their educational attainment and adult occupational status, regardless of differences in background characteristics between individuals.

Community colleges offer a different kind of college education. Type of college entered makes a difference in analyzing variation in adult occupational status, even when controlling for the effect of other background variables. Community college and four-year college education is not alike. How these differences shape adult socioeconomic status must be considered in status attainment models.

DISCUSSION

Community college entrants have achieved, on average, a lower occupational status than four-year college entrants after taking into account background differences. Regardless of subsequent educational history, beginning one's higher education at a community college versus a four-year college has a deleterious effect on adult status attainment. There is concern, therefore, that entering a community college rather than a four year college or university not only means it is less likely that one will eventually acquire the bachelor's degree but that should that goal be attained the community college entrant will not realize the same occupational return of their educational investment as will the four year college entrant.

For men, community college versus four year college entrance depresses occupational status. After taking into account differences in years of education completed, whether or not the bachelor's degree was awarded, measured ability, and other background variables, type of first college entered exerts an independent effect in shaping adult occupational status. Four-year college entrants realize an occupational benefit that comparable community college entrants never enjoy. In other words, the act of beginning one's higher education at a community college rather than a four year college or university entails an adult occupational penalty regardless of years of education acquired, ability, or other background variables.

The occupational return to each additional year of education is lower for female community college entrants than for female four-year college entrants. Compared to four-year college entrance, community college entrance depreciates the value of each additional year of education attained. In addition, the occupational return to acquisition of the bachelor's degree is lower for female community college entrants than for female four-year college entrants. On average, women are better off occupationally having entered a four-year college rather than a community college.

African American women experience a significant occupational benefit on completion of the bachelor's degree compared to African American women who do not finish the degree. African American women with the bachelor's degree enjoy a small occupational advantage over similarly trained white women. All women benefit socioeconomically by acquiring additional education. How community college entrance shapes educational outcomes merits further research attention.

Acquisition of the bachelor's degree appears critical for the occupational success of African American women. Given the high drop out rate from community colleges, African American women would be wise to consider the long term socioeconomic consequences of type of first college entered. If community college entrance has a depressive effect on years of education acquired and likelihood of completion of the bachelor's degree, and if African American women especially benefit from degree completion, then the decision to begin one's higher education at a community college rather than a four year college is not merely a decision of going to one college over another college. Rather, community college entrance entails an adult occupational penalty over four year college entrance all else equal.

On average, community college entrants achieve a lower occupational status than four-year college entrants all else equal. Regardless of ability, years of education acquired, bachelor's degree completion and other background variables, community college entrants never realize the same occupational return on their educational investment as a four year college entrant. Community colleges do not just provide two years of a college education; they provide a different kind of education compared to four year colleges or universities. Community college entrants may take courses that are not readily transferable to four-year institutions. This may mean it will take a longer time, as well as some frustration, for community college entrants compared to four year college entrants to complete the bachelor's degree. Tracking within community colleges may also influence the deleterious impact community college compared to four year college entrance has on adult occupational status. Again, even within non-vocational fields of study tracking is evident. How this shapes likelihood of persistence in the higher educational system as well as what happens during the transfer process is a rich area for further research. If our goal is to enhance occupational status via educational opportunity, then the socioeconomic consequences of differentiation in the structure of higher education must be further examined. Next, I turn and look at wage differences between community college and four year college entrants.

Economic Returns to Education: Do Rates of Return Vary Between Community and Four-Year College Entrants?

Economic Returns to Education: Do Rates of Return Vary
Between Community and Four-Year College Entrants?

Although almost half of all students enrolled in higher education are enrolled in a community college, there is little research on the economic effects of this decision. Early research analyzing correlations between educational attainment and earning ability virtually ignored the effects of community college entrance. Rather, educational experience was usually defined as number of years of schooling completed.[1] Where one acquired their education, at a community college, four year college, or university was not considered. Further, in analyzing returns to education, it was (and primarily still is) common practice to lump together all students with less than four years of a college education. Thus, community college dropouts, associate degree recipients, or four-year college dropouts were categorized together as they all had completed less than four years of college. Undoubtedly, there are differences between these individuals that should be considered in models aiming to unravel socioeconomic differences between adults.

In the recent past, a few analyzes have delved into the question how differentiation of higher education into sectors shapes economic returns to education. One of the better known of these is by Kane and Rouse. In their work, *"Labor Market Returns to Two- and Four-Year Colleges: Is a Credit a Credit and Do Degrees Matter?"*, they argue that wage returns to a college credit are similar between two- and four-year college entrants. They maintain that a college credit is a credit regardless of where a student acquired their education. [2] They excluded from their analysis those who were earning less than the minimum wage (in 1990) as well as those who earned over $72.00 an hour. Thus, their sample excludes individuals who are earning at the low or high extremes during their sample year 1990. On the other hand, others maintain economic returns do vary between comparable two- and four-year college entrants even after background differences have been taken into account. This is a critical question especially in light of the work of Ashenfelter and Krueger. In analyzing economic returns to education among a sample of identical twins with different schooling levels, they argue that past research underestimates economic returns to education. They estimate that the economic return to each year of education raises the wage rate by sixteen percent.[3] How this return may vary between two- and four-year college entrants, after differences in educational attainment and background variables have been taken into account, is critical to understanding wage differences in the United States today.

THE QUALITY ISSUE

To date, much of the literature that takes into account between school differences suggests that these differences account for little of the variation in educational performance, educational attainment, or earning ability.[4] These researchers conclude that differences in earning ability due to college effects are best understood by recognizing the nonrandom allocation of students to different types of colleges. They see selection and recruitment criteria as the real factors in the relationship between college differences and socioeconomic achievements. They maintain that ability, social class background, and college goal must be taken into account in analyzing differences in earning ability so that these background effects will not be wrongly attributed to the effect of college type. Therefore, in this work, the variables ability, socioeconomic status background, and whether or not an individual aims to finish the bachelor's degree, will be included as control variables in looking at the relationship between type of first college entered, educational attainment, and adult earning ability.

An additional problem with present literature that considers qualitative variations in educational experience is that quality has typically been defined in terms of per pupil expenditures. Quality has also been defined as the average schooling of teachers in the area in which an individual obtained their schooling. [5] Defining quality in either way ignores the fact that different kinds of higher educational institutions exist. Community colleges are four-year colleges cannot be properly treated as homogeneous. Differences must be recognized and analyzes should be done to see how these differences shape educational attainment and adult socioeconomic status attainment.

ECONOMIC RETURNS TO EDUCATION WITHIN A HUMAN CAPITAL MODEL

In this chapter, economic returns to education are analyzed between community college and four-year college entrants, with relevant background variables constant, for an age homogeneous population (27 years old) early in the life cycle. Differences in earning ability between community and four-year college entrants are drawn at age 27. I also project life-time earnings of each based on earning at age 27. This is a conservative analysis as one would expect the earnings gap between community and four-year college entrants to widen across time.

According to human capital theory, the breakeven point in analyzing variation in income between college graduates and high school graduates is about age 25. Labor economists draw age-earnings profiles by educational attainment. Their work shows that the earnings of college graduates are higher than the earnings of high school graduates. The peak earning period for college graduates is late in their fifties; the peak earning period for high school graduates is early in their forties. They account for this difference by suggesting the return to mental capital is higher and peaks later in the life cycle than the return to physical capital, which peaks early in the life cycle. [6]

Human capital theorists would expect to observe small differences in earning ability between community and four-year college entrants at age 27. Still, community college entrants should earn less, on average, than four-year college entrants (even with years of education constant) because they invested less in their education. In other words, community college entrants paid less for their education which entails a consequence as regards lifetime earning ability. A human capital theorist would *not* expect community college entrance to entail a wage penalty that is greater than would be predicted from differences in cost of the educational investment alone after taking into account background differences.

DIFFERENCES IN COLLEGE POPULATIONS

We must remember too that four year college entrants come from higher social class backgrounds as compared to community college entrants. Community college entrants come from lower social class backgrounds as measured by father's income, occupational status, and educational attainment, than four-year college entrants.[7] Almost half of the community college entrants in this sample are children of blue collar workers. Four year colleges draw twice as many of the children of professional and managerial workers compared to the community college. Differences in type of first college entered and father's income follow this pattern. The higher the father's income the more likely it is a student will first enter a four year rather than a community college.

The number of students whose father graduated from college differs between students who enter a community college and those who enter a four year college. Few of the fathers of students who enter a community college graduated from a four year college themselves. More than twice as many of the fathers of students who enter a four-year college, however, are college graduates. Nearly three-fourth's of the community college population comes from students whose father never entered college. For students whose father has done post-graduate work, it is more than twice as likely that they will enter a four year college instead of a community college.

The National Longitudinal Survey of Labor Market Experiences data support the contention that community college entrants come from lower social class backgrounds as measured by father's occupation, income, and educational attainment compared to four year college entrants. Type of first college entered in turns affects educational attainment and earning ability. Given that students from lower social class background disproportionately attend community college, how the differentiation of higher education into sectors shapes educational attainment is critical.

Most college entrants want to begin their higher education at a four year college and obtain the bachelors degree. Many community college entrants do not, as a human capital theorist might posit, freely choose the community college option. Rather, community college education may be the only way they can finance the first two years of a higher education. Given the vocational orientation of the community college and the 100 and 200-level course offerings, problems arise in the transfer process. Community colleges do not just offer the first two years of a college education. They offer a different kind of education. The community college system reflects an extension of class based tracking into higher education.

DESCRIPTIVE ANALYSIS

High school graduates in this sample have the most work experience. This makes sense as they have been in the labor force rather than continuing their formal education. Community and four year college dropouts have been working longer than bachelor degree recipients. Women, in this sample, who attained an associate's or bachelor's degree have one less year work experience on the average than does a comparable male. Once in the labor market, bachelor degree recipients work the longest hours.

Educational attainment shapes earning ability. Community college drop outs earn less than high school graduates (ten years after high school graduation). Bachelor degree recipients earn the most even though they have less work experience than others. On average, community college associate degree holders earn more than four year college drop outs. It must be remembered, though, that the odds are rather high against community college entrants completing either the associate's or bachelor's degree.

A larger earning differential exists between white male and female high school graduates and bachelor degree recipients than exists between African American male and female high school graduates and bachelor degree recipients. African American and white female bachelor degree recipients experience more of a wage advantage over comparable high school graduates, respectively, than is true for men. Higher education pays off for women as a group.

African American men earn less than white men regardless of educational attainment. African American men and all women, regardless of race, who have graduated from high school, dropped out of a community or a four year college, or earned the bachelor's degree, earn less than white male high school graduates. African American women and men benefit from more education, unless they drop out of a community college. By including categories for community college drop out and associate's degree recipients in analyzing income differences new insights can be gained in understanding the relationship between educational attainment and earning ability. However, in order to understand the independent effect type of college entered has on earning ability, one must hold constant other variables, such as years of education, ability, and socioeconomic background. Next, I turn to examine wage differences in this way.

ANALYSIS

Type of first college entered is a significant variable in shaping adult earning ability after controlling for differences in years of education, ability, and social origins. In other words, it makes a difference in how much money one will earn as an adult where they began their higher education. Four year college entrants gain a 6.4 percent wage advantage over community college entrants, all else being equal. Controlling for years of education eliminates one of the main effects of attending a community college, namely depressing educational attainment; therefore, my analysis yields a conservative test of the idea that type of college entered has an impact on adult earning ability.

ECONOMIC RETURNS AND IQ

Notably, mental ability is not a significant predictor of adult earning ability, all else equal. This result supports the work of Cohn and others.[8] Economic returns to education are not significantly affected by IQ, all else equal. Besides entering a four year college, living in a metropolitan area and out of the South also enhance adult earning ability.

ECONOMIC RETURNS AND GENDER

The return to an additional year of education is higher, on average, for women than for men. This difference is most apparent in analyzing earning differences when college entrants as well as high school graduates are included in the sample. In this case, the return to an additional year of education for women is 8 percent; for men, four percent. Women with a higher education experience more of a wage advantage over other women than is true for men.

A female college graduate has more lucrative occupational possibilities open to her than is true for a woman who did not go to college. Most female high school graduates who enter the labor force immediately after graduation take jobs as clerical or sales workers.[9] Female service and sales workers earn less money than male service or sales workers and less than female or male managers or professionals. The percentage difference between the earnings of male and female managers and professionals is also much lower than it is between male and female sales or service workers.[10] In others words, the wage gap is higher among sales and service workers than it is between managerial and professional workers. It should be noted too that male high school graduates who take jobs after graduation as a truck driver, salesperson, or construction worker typically earn more than female high school graduates. Undoubtedly, this relates to the types of jobs that are most easily open to these individuals.

Women may well benefit more than men by first entering a four year college rather than a community college. For women, the return to first entering a four year college instead of a community college is 7 percent; for men, 6 percent. Thus, while both men and women gain by entering a four year college instead of a community college, I posit that this relationship is more important for women as a group than for men.

ECONOMIC RETURNS TO YEARS OF EDUCATION BY TYPE OF FIRST COLLEGE ENTERED

Economic returns to an additional year of education are lower for community college than four year college entrants. For community college entrants, economic returns to an additional year of education are 5.4 percent a year; returns for four year college entrants are 7.9 percent a year. Thus, controlling for type of first college entered decreases the estimated returns to years of education. By not including a variable for type of first college entered, researchers analyzing earning differences overestimate the return to years of education. A community college entrants who acquires four years of a college education never realizes as high an economic return on this investment as will a four year college entrant.

PROJECTED LIFETIME COST DIFFERENCES BETWEEN COMMUNITY COLLEGE ENTRANTS AND FOUR YEAR COLLEGE ENTRANTS

There is much more of a wage benefit associated with entering a four year college than the cost saved by entering a community college. By 1996, it cost $7,013 a year, on average, to attend a public four year college or university, and $4,236 to attend a public community college.[11] Thus, an individual saves $2,777 a year, for two years, (the institutional cost difference) by entering a community college rather than a four year college. The present value of the added income stream of four year college entrants (with four years of a college education) at the time of first entering college, given an 8% discount rate, is $9,300. This is a conservative calculation as the earning differential between community and four year college entrants with the same number of years of education is assumed to remain the same throughout the life cycle (for the purpose of my example) as it was at age 27. Most likely, the gap between the community and four year college entrant, even with years of education constant, will grow over the life cycle. In dollar terms, it does not make sense to enter a community college. Instead of saving money, in the long run, the community college entrant is heavily penalized.

DISCUSSION

Type of first college entered is a significant variable in shaping adult earning ability even after differences in years of education acquired, mental ability, socioeconomic and other background variables have been taken into account. Mental ability is not a significant predictor of adult earning ability net of other factors. When controlling of first college entered, the return to each year of education declines. In other words, each year of additional education is not worth the same for community and four year college entrants. Community college entrants do not realize the same economic return on their educational investment as will a four year college entrant. It would be wise for researchers to take into account not only years of education by also type of first college entered in analyzing economic returns to education.

The return to each year of education is lower for community than four year college entrants. Community college entrants with the same number of years of education as four year entrants never realize the same economic gains. Community college entrance entails a wage penalty that is greater than would be predicted from cost of the educational investment alone. In the long run, it cost more money to enter a community college than a four year college. The income loss, over the life course, for community college entrants (given the lower return to each additional year of education) is much higher than the initial cost saved by attending a two year institution.

Another Look at The Economic Returns to Education and Degrees

Another Look At The Economic Returns

To Education And Degrees[1]

As we have seen, it is generally accepted that acquiring the bachelor's degree enhances adult earning ability.[2] Studies have shown, though, that having part of a four-year college education is of limited economic value.[3] Given the increase in the number of and enrollment in community colleges, it is important to analyze economic rates of return by both years of education achieved and by type of degree earned.

To date, research results on the economic returns to community and four year educational investments are mixed. For example, in their work Kane and Rouse maintain that two-year and four-year college credits are worth roughly the same as regards economic returns. They go on to argue that the economic value of having the bachelor's degree is of small relevance compared to the number of credits completed.[4] Alternatively, Jaeger and Page posit "sheepskin" effects hold. In other words, acquiring a degree has a positive effect on adult economic attainment. However, Jaeger and Page dot not find significant differences in economic returns to the bachelor's degree by race or gender. They do find that white women who complete the associate's degree benefit more than do comparable men.[5]

In the last chapter, we saw that community college entrants earned less, on average, than four-year college entrants, all else equal, in part because they invest less in their education. Further, the community college educational investment may be a signal to employers that an individual comes from a particular socioeconomic background. This information may be used as a sorting device as regards decisions relating to earning ability that differentially impacts community versus four year college students.[6] Thus, if an employer has a bias against community college education, they may act on this information, knowingly or not, in a way that negatively impacts economic opportunities for the community college entrant.

In this chapter, economic returns to education, by years of education completed and type of degree attained, will be analyzed for a sample of women and men early in the life cycle. In the last chapter, economic returns to education were analyzed for individuals who had been out of high school ten years. This sample consists of employed individuals all of whom graduated from high school. Their average age is 27.[7] Thus, it is a current youth survey. How wage differences appear between those with an associate's degree and a bachelor's degree adds additional insight into how the differentiation of higher education into sectors shapes life opportunities. In addition, economic returns to vocational education will be explored. How well are individuals doing economically, on average, who have acquired a vocational degree compared to others?

VOCATIONAL EDUCATION

By the early 1990s, approximately four million students were enrolled in vocational courses at non-collegiate schools and 37 percent of these students worked full time. This enrollment includes business, vocational, technical, secretarial, trade, or correspondence courses which are not counted as regular school enrollment and are not for recreational or adult education.[8] The cost of taking a vocational class at a non-collegiate school is roughly comparable to what it costs to take a class at a community college.[9] Among community college students, over half (approximately 66 percent) are in a vocational or technical rather than an academic or transfer program.[10]

Vocational education, both at the community college and at non-collegiate institutions, is critical to teaching and certifying technical skills because apprenticeship type learning is rare. For example, in the United States today there are approximately 400,000 individuals in apprenticeships.[11] The percentage of female apprenticeships remains low. The same situation holds true for minority members.[12]

The importance of vocational education must be seen in light of changing labor market opportunities. Robert Reich believes that the days when skilled or low-skilled workers could find "good paying factory jobs for life are gone".[13]   The shift from industry to service continues to characterize the United States economy. While some job growth is expected in the skilled trades, service work remains the fastest growing occupational group. Within the service occupations, the fastest growing occupations will be those that require the most formal education and training.[14]   These occupations include: technicians and related support, professional specialties, service, executive and administrative work, marketing as well as sales occupations.[15]

Service occupations, projected to grow faster than average, cover a wide range. Service occupations include paid household work, commercial food and drink preparation and service, the providing of lodging and related services, provision of grooming, cosmetic and other personal health care services, clothes maintenance and cleaning, and protective services.   Service industries, the largest sector of the economy, employ managerial, professional, clerical, and other types of workers. During the last decade, the number of women working in service occupations increased substantially. This trend held despite the sharp decline in the number of domestic workers. A larger proportion of employed women (19 percent) than men (10 percent) hold service jobs.[16]

The community college associate degree in applied science (A.A.S.) is primarily directed at training service workers. Degree programs include: public service technology (including the police, early childhood teachers, and fire science), health technology (nursing, physical therapy assistant), arts and design technology, and business technology (hotel and restaurant management). Certificate programs in the community college also train and certify people to enter service and trade jobs.

How these students, who choose a vocational degree, fare in the work world, especially in terms of earnings, deserves further research attention. By comparing economic outcomes of vocational degree students to others, the benefits and drawbacks to vocational education will be better understood. This is especially important in light of President Clinton's Goals 2000 program. This program, which plans to combine high school with vocational education, aims to certify students with a marketable skill.[17]

Economic returns to years of education, and how this may vary by both race and gender, are also examined. Specifically, how does the economic return to each additional year of education or degree attained differ between women and men and African Americans and whites after background variables have been taken into account. I expect to observe significant differences in economic returns to additional years of education by race. In their work, Bound and Freeman explore the erosion of relative earnings among young black men in the 1980s.[18] Thus, white men should enjoy an economic advantage over comparable black men given, in part, structural problems facing African American men in the labor market. If economic returns to education significantly differ by race, this would not negate the importance of acquiring additional years of education. If anything, young black men would need an educational advantage just to keep a competitive edge in the labor market. Again, how community college entrance may shape educational attainment, which impacts adult socioeconomic status, is especially important to better understand in status attainment models that delve into differences by race.

I do not expect to observe significant differences in economic returns to the associate's degree by gender. An increasing number of researchers including, Pincus, Valez, and Karabel, generally find that community college education is, as Dougherty writes, a hindrance not an aid to socioeconomic success.[19] I expect to observe in this sample, as held in the earlier sample of people who have been out of high school ten years, that the economic return to community college education is of limited benefit.

ANALYSIS

After taking into account differences in age, mental ability, sex, race, as well as other background variables, the economic return for each additional year of education an individual achieves increases their hourly wage by 1.9 percent. As expected whites earn more than others all else equal. Whites enjoy a 10 percent wage advantage, on average, compared to others. Men earn 9 percent more, on average, than do women.

RETURNS TO DEGREES

Having an associate's degree adds 5 percent to a person's earnings, however, this is not a statistically significant difference. Thus, there is no "sheepskin" effect associated with the associate's degree. Likewise, the economic benefit to having a vocational degree, at least at this point in the life cycle, does not hold in this work. An associate's degree recipient or vocational degree recipient is no better off economically than if they had entered the labor market immediately after high school graduation.

On the other hand, having the bachelor's degree yields a significant economic return. Those with a bachelor's degree earn 10 percent more than high school graduates without the degree. If the bachelor's recipient also has four additional years of education over a high school graduate, they will receive about 7.6 percent more from the additional years of education (plus the 10 percent for having the bachelor's degree). In total, a bachelor's degree recipient receives about 18% more than the high school graduate without any further education. Remember, too, that this is at an early stage in the life cycle. If anything, the gap between the two will widen over time.

Besides years of education and holding the bachelor's degree, being male, white, older, having more work experience, living outside the South, living in a standard metropolitan statistical area, being married, and having the bachelor's degree as an educational goal are positively associated with higher wages. These general results are in line with the work of others who analyze socioeconomic returns to education.[20] Next, I turn and look at how economic returns to education vary by race and gender.

ESTIMATED ECONOMIC RETURNS TO THE BACHELOR'S DEGREE BY GENDER AND RACE

Among people in this sample, white men with a bachelor's degree and four years of a college education earned 22.5 percent more than comparable high school graduates.[21] Similarly, white women with the bachelor's degree and four years of a college education earned 24.5 percent more than white female high school graduates. African American men with a bachelor's degree and four years of a college education earned 13.1 percent more than comparable high school graduates. African American women with the bachelor's degree and four years of college earned 15.3 percent more than African American women that just finished high school. Thus, white and African American women with the bachelor's degree and four years of college earn a little more relatively over comparable high school graduates than holds for white or African American men. Given that many maintain that the United States labor market is characterized by greater sex, than race, segregation then the importance of education in shaping the adult socioeconomic status of women is critical to better understand.[22]

THE WAGE GAP

Among people in this sample, the estimated expected earnings of white women with a bachelor's degree and four years of college compared to a comparable white man is $ .73 to the dollar; for African American women the wage gap is $ .75 to the dollar. In other words, African American women earned, on average, 75 cents to every dollar earned by a comparable African American man. These figures are in line with the overall wage gap that currently holds in the United States labor market. Currently, women earn, on average, 74 cents to every dollar a man earns.[23] Some expect the wage gap to narrow by the year 2000, "no one expects it to disappear in the foreseeable future."[24]

The wage gap in the United States has been wide and persistent. The current wage gap is an improvement over recent years. For example, in 1955, women's median earnings as a percent of men's were 63.9 percent; in 1978, 59 percent; in 1985, 64 percent.[25] Women are over-represented among workers whose earnings are low and under-represented among workers whose earnings are high. The wage gap was first documented in the United States in 1815, when the earnings of women in agriculture were 28.8 percent of the earnings of men in agriculture.[26]

Analysts suggest that the wage gap narrowed because of the gains women have made in entering higher paid male-dominated occupations. Still, the wage gap in the United States is much wider than in many European countries. For example, in Italy women's median earnings as a percent of men's are approximately 86 percent; in France, 78 percent; in Denmark, 86 percent.[27] Perhaps the slow progress in reducing sex differentials in earnings in the United States exists, in part, because many women begin their higher education at a community college. Channeling large numbers of women into two year colleges perpetuates occupational sex segregation and keeps women's wages low by depressing educational attainment.[28] More work needs to examine the link between community college entrance, educational attainment, occupational segregation, and the wage gap.

DISCUSSION

Differences in log hourly wages among full time employed men and women, for a youth sample, are analyzed. The average age of the sample is 27, therefore, wage differences are analyzed early in the life cycle. Differences in earning ability and returns to degrees, particularly the associate's and bachelor's degrees, are explored. Each additional year of education past high school yields an economic return of 1.9 percent. Only bachelor degree recipients enjoy an economic advantage on completion of the degree (10%); associate and vocational degree holders do not significantly benefit from a sheepskin effect. Thus, people with a bachelor's degree earn 10 percent more than high school graduates without a degree. If the bachelor's recipient also has four years of education more than a high school graduate with no further education, they will receive about 8 percent more from years of education (plus the 10 percent for the bachelor's degree). In total, bachelor degree recipients receive about 18 percent more than high school graduates without any further education. Besides years of education and the bachelor's degree, being white, male, older, having more work experience, living outside the South, being in a standard metropolitan statistical area, married, and having the bachelor's degree as an educational goal are all positively associated with higher wages.

Community College Entrance: Better Than Not Going to College at All?

Community College Entrance: Better Than Not Going to College at All?[1]

Recently, increasing numbers of investigators have looked at the socioeconomic consequences of community college attendance. Most of these studies examine the benefit of beginning one's higher education at a four year college or university compared to a community college. Studies by Karabel, Alwin, Breneman and Nelson, Alba and Lavin, Anderson, and Dougherty generally report that, compared to four year college entrance, community college entrance has a deleterious effect on adult socioeconomic attainment.[2] In other words, beginning one's higher education at a community college, rather than a four year college or university, entails a penalty in terms of either educational attainment, adult earning ability, or adult occupational status attainment. This effect is largely attributed to the poorer educational investment by community college entrants, the depressive effect community college entrance exerts on years of schooling acquired, and the "second best" image surrounding community college institutions.[3] Zwerling characterized the image many have of community college education. Namely, it is not the first college choice for many but a perceived attractive alternative primarily for economic considerations and convenience. Neither community college students nor instructors are perceived in the same way as are four year college and university students and faculty. A perceived quality difference between community and four year college education is evident in the minds of many.

Here, I empirically assess the benefit, in terms of both occupational status and earning ability, of going to a community college instead of not going to college at all. In contrast to previous studies, this work examines differences in adult occupational status and earning ability between community college entrants compared to those who entered the labor force after high school graduation.[4] For an additional point of comparison, socioeconomic differences are also drawn between four year college entrants and high school graduates. Socioeconomic differences between community and four year college dropouts will also be compared with others. Virtually all current work on the socioeconomic consequences of community college entrance compare community and four year college entrants. In earlier chapters, we have seen that community college entrance entails a socioeconomic penalty compared to four year college entrance. Now, I explore whether or not going to a community college is better than not going to college at all. In other words, is one better off socioeconomically if they enter a community college, and/or acquire the two year associate's degree, compared to entering the labor force immediately after high school graduation.

AFTER HIGH SCHOOL GRADUATION: DIFFERENT PATHS

Nationally, approximately half of all high school graduates enter the labor market immediately after graduation.[5] Among college entrants, approximately half enter community colleges while others go to four year colleges or universities. Of those who enter a community college, approximately 21 percent acquire the two year associate's degree. This is the terminal degree offered by community college institutions. For the vast majority of associate degree holders, this is their terminal degree.[6] In other words, the two year associate's degree is the highest degree ever achieved.

Among four year college entrants, it is generally accepted that completion of the fourth year of college and acquisition of the bachelor's degree are important factors in shaping adult socioeconomic achievements. Higher education affords one certain skills that others, who did not pursue such an education, do not have to offer potential employers in the job search process. Further, the degree provides a signal to employers regarding an individual's social and educational background.[7] Having a four year college degree is generally perceived as a positive good. Taking a functionalist position, a college graduate is in a position to enter jobs deemed by the society as those that are most important to the working of the society as a whole. In order to induce people to pursue the education necessary to enter such jobs, the prospect of a high wage must be there. Likewise, human capital theorists posit that those who acquire a higher education have invested more in their "human capital" and the return on this investment will be significant. Otherwise, a human capital theorist is at a loss to explain why one would undertake advanced training and education. Such a pursuit is not generally conceived with the model as pleasurable activity.

Community college critics have long argued that community college entrance is not a perfect substitute for admission at a four year college or university.[8] Pincus makes the point that community colleges may offer students an opportunity to try but not an opportunity to succeed.[9] Compared to the four year college environment, community colleges offer, on average, fewer mentors and encouragement, less rigorous lower-level college classes, and less of an expectation (on the part of both students and teachers) that students will succeed.[10] Among baccalaureate aspirants, community college entrants attain less educationally and economically than comparable four year college entrants. Given these differences, I expect that community college entrants, even those who go on to acquire the bachelor's degree, will not enjoy the same socioeconomic advantages four year bachelor degree recipients realize.

Little research analyzes the socioeconomic status of associate degree holders compared to others.[11] Nonetheless, community college supporters tout the benefits of the two year associate's degree.[12] It seems reasonable to hypothesize that the benefit of having this credential does not carry the same value in our society as having completed the bachelor's degree. Further, it is generally accepted that having part of a college education does not significantly enhance adult socioeconomic status. Thus, the net benefit of acquiring the two year associate's degree may be modest.

The socioeconomic status of community and four year college dropouts should be no better, possible worse, than those who entered the labor market immediately after high school graduation. Dropouts gain no higher credential past high school. Further, they lack the work experience high school graduates gain on the job. Little research, though, looks at possible socioeconomic differences between community and four year college dropouts. For example, how do four year college dropouts fare compared to associate degree recipients? This work examines the socioeconomic benefit of the associate's degree compared to those who dropped out of college and never acquired a credential at all. Perhaps, four year college dropouts will be doing better socioeconomically than community college dropouts. Given insights from signaling theory, four year college dropouts would at least have the advantage of having been accepted to a four year college or university. The expectation was there that they could have acquired the bachelor's degree. No such assumption holds in the case of community college dropouts. If anything, dropping out of a community college may be worse than not entering the higher educational system at all. This status may be a double negative in that an individual entered a community college and additionally that they dropped out of college. A potential employer might well see this outcome as a red flag that may signal problems the individual could experience in the workplace as well as in the higher educational system.

This work examines socioeconomic differences ten years after high school graduation. Again, socioeconomic differences are drawn at a point early in the life cycle. Further, socioeconomic differences are drawn, for this sample, during a historical period, shortly prior to the 1980s, when the economic return to higher education was depressed. The large well educated baby boom cohort flooded the labor market which depressed economic returns to higher education. Thus, the wage gap between college educated individuals and those with a high school certificate narrowed. Individuals had to have an advanced education, and often a degree, to acquire a job that earlier had no such entrance requirement. There was a period of inflation for education and advanced degrees.

Levy and Murnane maintain that the current economic return to education is 16 percent or approximately double what the economic return to education was in the 1970s and early 1980s.[13] Returns to education during this earlier time period were depressed. Thus, this work allows a rigorous test of socioeconomic returns to years of education and degrees between community college entrants and others. If differences appear at this point in time, then during a time period when economic returns to education are high, one would expect to observe even greater differences socioeconomically between community college entrants and others.

I expect to observe marked differences in occupational status between college entrants and others. Namely, I believe that four year college entrants will enjoy a higher occupational status compared to others. I think this advantage will hold over community college entrants who transfer to finish the four year bachelor's degree. In this work, occupational status is measured on the Duncan index. The index ranges from 0 to 96. The higher the score, the more prestigious the occupation. Given a possible gender bias in its construction, coupled with concern in regard to how reliable this index is in discerning occupational prestige differences by gender, socioeconomic differences here will be restricted to males.[14] For example, many women fall in the category of clerical or sales worker. These occupations are ranked high on the Duncan index, whereas, an occupation a man may enter who has a similar educational background might be construction. Construction is not ranked as a very prestigious occupation on this index.

While the economic pay off to education was depressed during the period I examine, occupational status differences between college entrants and others continued to characterize the labor market. In other words, college entrants had access to higher prestige occupations compared to high school graduates, even though the economic returns to the higher status jobs were depressed.[15] Thus, I expect to observe marked differences in occupational status between community college entrants compared to others.

Because of possible interaction effects between the variables race and region in shaping occupational and earning differences, several interaction terms are included in this work. Therefore, I examine how occupational status and earning ability vary between African American and white men who live in the South compared to out of the South. Also, I look at how socioeconomic differences vary by race and whether or not a person lives in a standard metropolitan statistical area. Link and Ratledge argue that it is more advantageous, in terms of both occupational status and wages, for African American men, compared to white men, to live outside the South rather than in the South.[16] They find that the effect of race discrimination in the labor market is not as evident outside of the South as holds in the South. The evidence of a socioeconomic advantage for living in a standard metropolitan statistical area for African American compared to white men is mixed.[17] In other words, some researchers find that African American men do benefit socioeconomically from living in a standard metropolitan statistical area; other researchers find no such statistically significant effect.

DESCRIPTIVE ANALYSIS

In this sample, 42 percent of respondents are high school graduates who never entered college. Rather, these individuals entered the labor market immediately after high school graduation. Of those who went to college, approximately 29 percent entered a community college while 71 percent began their higher education at a four year school. Thus, compared to the general population, fewer people in my sample entered community colleges while more entered four year colleges. Approximately a third of community college entrants dropped out of school by the end of the second year of college. Compared to figures for the general population, this is a low dropout rate for community college entrants in my sample. Among four year college entrants, a third had dropped out by the end of their four year in school. Approximately 18 percent of community college entrants in my sample acquired the associate's degree. The majority (67 percent) of four year entrants and almost half (48 percent) of community college entrants acquired the bachelor's degree.

OCCUPATIONAL STATUS DIFFERENCES

The occupational status of community college entrants who acquired the associate's degree, community and four year college entrants who acquired the bachelor's degree, and four year entrants who dropped out of college is higher than the occupational status of high school graduates. Having a degree, whether or not it is an associate's degree or a bachelor's degree, is beneficial occupationally compared to entering the labor market immediately after high school graduation. The occupational return to four year college entrants who acquire the bachelor's degree is significantly higher than community college associate degree holders or community college bachelor recipients or four year college drop outs. Thus, in terms of occupational status four year college entrants who acquired the bachelor's degree are in a more advantageous position than are comparable community college entrants. Even if the two acquire the same amount of education, and the same degree, where they began their education impacts adult occupational status.

As hypothesized, the occupational return to community college associate degree recipients is not significantly higher than the occupational return to four year college dropouts. In other words, having the associate's degree does not benefit one occupationally, compared to entering the labor force immediately after high school graduation, at least at this point in the life cycle. In looking at occupational differences, there is no significant difference in how well four year college dropouts are doing compared to those who acquired the two year associate's degree.

The socioeconomic benefit to the associate's degree is modest. There is no empirical evidence that the occupational status of community college dropouts is any better (or worse) than high school graduates. In other words, a community college entrant who fails to acquire the associate's degree or who never transfers to complete the bachelor's degree is no better off occupationally than is a high school graduate who entered the labor market immediately after completion of twelve years of formal schooling. For this sample, occupational status is also generally enhanced by growing older, increased mental ability, coming from a higher socioeconomic class background, living in a standard metropolitan statistical area, living in the South, being married, and being white. These general findings are in line with the findings of others who examine socioeconomic returns to education.

RACE DIFFERENCES IN OCCUPATIONAL STATUS ATTAINMENT

I find that living in a standard metropolitan statistical area is more advantageous occupationally for white than African American men. White men enhance their occupation status should they live in a standard metropolitan statistical area, whereas the occupational status of African American men is negatively impacted by living in an urban area. I also examined occupational differences between African American and white men who live in the South compared to out of the South. I find that, African American men fare better, in terms of occupational status, than white men should they live outside the South. African American men who live outside the South enhance their occupational status, whereas white men do not benefit occupationally by living outside the South. These results are in line with the work of others who find less occupational discrimination by race outside of the South than elsewhere.[18] The occupational return to African American men who live outside the South, and in a standard metropolitan statistical area, is not significantly different from comparable white men.

WAGE DIFFERENCES

Differences in hourly wage were also examined between high school graduates and college entrants. Data show that earning ability is enhanced by growing older, higher measured mental ability, coming from a higher socioeconomic background, living in a standard metropolitan statistical area, living outside of the South, being married, not having children, and being white. There is no statistically significant evidence in this work that dropping out of a community college helps (or hurts) the occupational prestige or earning ability of full time employed adult men. In other words, high school graduates who entered the labor market immediately after graduation are doing about the same, in terms of occupational status attainment, as are those who entered a community college and dropped out.

Earlier we saw that white four year college dropouts enjoyed an occupational advantage over high school graduates. There is no evidence, in my work, that they enjoy a wage benefit as well. Notably, there is no empirical evidence that community college entrants who acquire the associate's degree enjoy a wage benefit over others. Thus, associate degree holders are doing no better or worse, as regards adult earning ability, than are those who entered the labor market immediately after high school graduation. It appears that the economic value of having this degree does not carry the same value in our society as completing the four year bachelor's degree. There is no sheepskin effect associate with attaining the associate's degree at least there is no such effect at this point in the life cycle.

Only community and four year college bachelor degree recipients experience a wage advantage over high school graduates and others. There is no evidence in this work that the economic return to the bachelor's degree is significantly different between community and four year college entrants. Thus, while four year college entrants with the bachelor's degree enjoy a significantly higher occupational status compared to community college entrants with the same degree, this occupational benefit did not translate to a wage benefit. How this difference will shape life opportunities of comparable community and four year college entrants over time is worthy of further investigation.

DISCUSSION

Is going to a community college better than not going to college at all? Community college entrants who acquire the associate's or bachelor's degree enjoy a higher occupational status than those who entered the labor market after graduating from high school. Among four year college entrants, both dropouts and bachelor degree recipients fare better occupationally than high school graduates. This does not hold true for community college dropouts. Community college dropouts are doing no better occupationally than are those who entered the labor market immediately after high school graduation.

There is no evidence in this work that the occupational return to the associate's degree is significantly different that the occupational return to dropping out of a four year college. One appears to have the same occupational consequence as the other. Notably, four year college bachelor degree recipients enjoy a significantly higher occupational return compared to community college bachelor degree recipients. Nevertheless, the economic return between community college and four year college bachelor degree recipients is not significantly different. In other words, at this point in the life cycle, community college bachelor degree recipients are doing as well as those who acquired the bachelor's degree who started their higher education at a four year college or university. Community college dropouts are doing no better (or worse) socioeconomically compared to high school graduates. Thus, for many community college entrants the benefit from their educational choice is the college experience itself. It is important to remember that the majority of community college entrants eventually drop out of the higher educational system. What kind of socioeconomic returns they enjoy, or do not enjoy, is something that is important in the lives of many students. Likewise, for community college entrants who attain the associate's degree, perhaps the occupational benefit they enjoy from this educational accomplishment provides a positive utility regardless of the wage effect. Community college associate degree recipients are doing no better in terms of adult earning ability than are those who entered the labor market immediately after high school graduation. Again, how this difference shapes labor market opportunities for associate degree holders is something to track over time.

With respect to wages, community and four year college entrants who acquire the bachelor's degree are doing significantly better than others. There is no significant economic return to the associate's degree. Having the associate's degree, in itself, is not a significant predictor of adult earning ability. In fact, achieving the associate's degree may have a deleterious impact on acquisition of additional years of education, and the bachelor's degree, which appears critical to enhancing the earning ability of community college entrants.

Conclusion

In this work, I reviewed three theories of educational experience and labor market outcomes. These theories included functionalism, human capital and conflict. Functional and human capital theory emphasize ability and choice in educational attainment and career opportunities. Conflict theory stresses the importance of social class background and educational differentiation in the determination of adult socioeconomic status. I argue that neither functional theory nor human capital theory can adequately deal with the significance of the differentiation of higher education into sectors. Such differentiation brings into question problems of conflict and social class. My findings are consistent with more radical critiques of the community college. The work of Bowles and Gintis, Jerome Karabel, and Fred Pincus also falls in this realm.

Community colleges are not the avenues for upward mobility that their supporters claim. Community colleges, I believe, are an extension of a class based tracking system into higher education. How my findings support this argument are outlined here.

FUNCTIONALISM AND HUMAN CAPITAL THEORY

In educational research, functionalism and human capital theory stress the efficient use of human resources. Since human resources are not to be wasted, these theories lend support to the idea of equality of opportunity. They emphasize ability, choice, skill and investment in education. Economists and sociologists see investment in education and socioeconomic returns to education significantly linked. The individual is viewed as a conscious decision maker who chooses among many available options to invest in those that will most likely yield the greatest future benefits. How well reality matches these theoretical assumptions is, of course, open for debate.

Most researchers recognize that not all individuals have an equal opportunity to enter the higher educational system which shapes adult socioeconomic status. Effects of discrimination are, therefore, important aspects of research analyzing socioeconomic differences by educational attainment. With the rise of community colleges, formal equality of access into the higher educational system became a reality for larger numbers of individuals. Taking a functional or human capital perspective, one could argue that an individual chose to enter a community college. Given this decision, they have an opportunity to try to succeed educationally. If community colleges were two year institutions of higher education geared to transfer, then such a perspective would not be so problematic. To focus on choice and free will in access to opportunity, however, clouds the issue of how educational differentiation relates to equality of outcomes. Jerome Karabel's work is central to better understanding these issues. Karabel examines the composition of the community and four year college populations as well as how educational outcomes differ between those who began their higher education at different types of institutions.

Early studies analyzing the relationship between social class background, educational experience, and labor market outcomes showed social class as a major determinant of the length and quality of education individuals obtained.[1] This view has gradually been supplanted by one that emphasize the importance of an independent effect of education on socioeconomic status. This leads to the idea that education is a way to overcome the influence of social class background on career opportunities. I argue that type of first college entered, which is shaped by an individual's social class background, tends to reinforce class effects on educational attainment and adult socioeconomic status. In establishing the community college, our society has created an institution that is an important link in the transmission of inequality from generation to generation. Those with fewer economic resources, as well as those who score more poorly on IQ type tests, are more likely than others to enter a community college rather than a four year college or university. Tracking large numbers of such nontraditional students into community colleges, I argue, tends to reinforce class divisions within the society as a whole.

THE COMMUNITY COLLEGE POPULATION

Community college entrants come from lower social class backgrounds as measured by father's education, father's occupation, and father's income, than four year college entrants.[2]   In my sample, twice as many of the fathers of four year college entrants as community college entrants are college graduates or have done post graduate work. Twice as many of the fathers of four year college entrants as community college entrants are professionals or managers. Half of the community college entrants come from families where the father is a low income earner; most four year college entrants come from families where the father earns a significantly higher income. The composition of the community college student body is notably different from that of a four year college. What happens to a student once the decision has been made to enter a community college is critically important.

EDUCATIONAL OUTCOMES

Nationally, more than half of community college entrants drop out of college. In this sample, less than a third of those who entered a four-year college dropped out of school. Dropping out of a community college is problematic because of the high numbers of individuals involved as well as socioeconomic consequences of this event. In this sample, community college dropouts earn less than high school graduates ten years after high school graduation. There is more of a wage disadvantage associated with dropping out of a community college than a four year college. Four year college entrants tend to stay in college and finish the bachelor's degree. Over half of the students who entered a four year college, in my sample, achieved the bachelor's degree. On the other hand, less than a third of those who entered a community college transferred to obtain the bachelor's degree. Even when community college entrants transfer to finish the bachelor's degree, their adult occupational status is not as high, on average, as that of comparable four year college entrants. Community college entrants who obtain the two year associate's degree earn more than four year college dropouts; however, relatively few community college entrants obtain the associate's degree.

Individuals from lower socioeconomic backgrounds and those who score lower on IQ type tests, are hurt more socioeconomically by entering a community college than a four year college. My work shows that the effects of socioeconomic background and ability are more important in understanding income differences for community college entrants than four year college entrants holding constant all other variables in the model including years of education. Analyzing wage regressions for the sample as a whole and for a sub-sample of college entrants, I find that women and nonwhites are hurt the most socioeconomically by first entering a community college rather than a four year college or university. The economic return to entering a four year college rather than a community college is higher for women compared to men and nonwhites compared to whites. Further, the return to an additional year of education is less for women and for nonwhites after taking into consideration type of first college entered. Women and nonwhites both benefit socioeconomically from additional education perhaps more so than for men or for whites as a group. Since four year college entrance is associated with the likelihood of completing additional education as well as acquisition of the bachelor's degree, then it is especially important for women and nonwhites to consider consequences of the choice to enter a community college institution. Looking at the long run picture, the immediate gain one may receive by entering a community college, primarily lower tuition costs and convenience, is not great enough to overcome the socioeconomic cost of this choice in terms of adult socioeconomic opportunity. Community college entrance may hurt most the nontraditional students (nonwhites, women, and those from less advantaged socioeconomic backgrounds) it purportedly aims to serve.

COMMUNITY AND FOUR YEAR COLLEGE INSTITUTIONS

In the past thirty years, the community college system has developed faster than any other sector of higher education. In 1963, for example, there were only 634 two year colleges. That figure had increased to 1,284 by 1995. The growth in the number of community colleges has brought more students into the community college system too. The growth in the number of institutions has been for public institutions rather than private ones.

In the early 1960s, there were only 844,512 community college students; by 1985, this figure had increased to 4,270,000 students. Enrollment in two year colleges doubled between the years 1970 and 1985, a change of 112 percent, while enrollment in four year colleges increased by only 21 percent. Today, 48 percent of all students enrolled in higher education are at community colleges not four year institutions. For large numbers of students, community colleges are the point of entry into the higher educational system.

By 1978, more women than men were enrolled in community colleges. Minority students are also more likely to enter community colleges than are white students. The community college system grew so much, in part, to meet the challenge of increased college enrollments in the 1960s. Community colleges are generally perceived as transfer oriented institutions. Attending a community college is less expensive than entering a four year college. Four year colleges and universities did not open their doors to all. Instead, community colleges emerged to fill a need. Is community college education, though, really a good alternative to entering a four year college? Are these two types of institutions interchangeable.

WORDS OF CAUTION

Most community college entrants want to transfer to a four year college. Few community college entrants, though, actually transfer. For many, this is the most troublesome consequence of first entering a community college rather than a four year institution. This is evidenced by words of caution published in 1997 by the Department of Education suggesting that "although attending a community college may make good financial sense, it may not be conducive to completing a bachelor's degree."[3] Isn't it incredible for the Department of Education to be cautioning students against entering an official tier within the United States higher educational system. How many students, one imagines, has read or heard this advise? If they have read this piece of advise, how many feel they have another option in their pursuit of an advanced higher education?

The community college is a place where many students reach undesired destinations. Burton Clark coined the term 'cooling out' to refer to the process whereby community college students who want to transfer but are not perceived as having the ability to do so come to see heir first choice as inappropriate; instead, they drop out or go into a vocational field.[4] The dilemma of the role of community colleges, Clark argues, is that the cooling out function should not be understood by prospective students; otherwise, the ability of the community college to perform this function would be impaired. If prospective community college entrants understood its function, pressure for college admission would turn back on four year colleges and universities. How well could these institutions absorb additional numbers of students?

Compared to four year college entrance, community college entrance has a negative impact on college completion. Community colleges are not the most advantageous places to start one's higher education. The most likely outcome of first entering a community college is dropping out of the higher educational system.

ECONOMIC COST DIFFERENCES AND RETURNS TO EDUCATION

It is less expensive to begin one's higher education at a community college and to transfer to complete the last two years of a college education than to first enter a four year college. Or is it? In order to calculate this saving, of first entering a community college, I offer the following example. I will assume that an individual goes to a community college for two years and transfers to obtain a bachelor's degree. That individual will have saved the cost of attending a four year college for two years and can invest the saving in something besides education. It costs approximately $7,013 a year to attend a public four year college and $4,236 a year to attend a community college. An individual would save $2,777 a year (for two years) by entering a community college. Compounding interest on the savings of $5,554, at a rate of 8%, a community college entrant will have $11,987 at the end of ten years. Assuming that this individual invests this money at a rate of 8%, they will draw approximately $959.00 each year. This is the opportunity cost of entering a four year college instead of a community college. Economists think of opportunity costs as the cost of the foregone alternative. Four year college entrants must invest more financially up front in their education. They do not reap the savings that community college entrants realize by investing in a less expensive educational alternative.

To calculate the benefit to entering a four year college, I offer the following example. In 1996, high school graduates earned approximately $24,000 annually. In analyzing economic returns by type of college entered, I found that the rate of return to an additional year of education for community college entrants was 5 percent; for four year college entrants 8 percent. Therefore, on average a four year college entrant, with four years of a college education, would earn $32,640 (in 1996 dollars) a year; a comparable community college entrants would earn only $29,170 a year. Four year college entrants, again with four years of a college education, earn $3,470 more *a year* than comparable community college entrants. It is safe to say that this figure will increase over time. Thus, there is much more of a wage benefit associated with entering a four year college ($3,470 a year) than the opportunity cost saved by entering a community college ($959.00 a year). In dollars terms, it does not make sense to enter a community college. Instead of saving money, in the long run the community college entrant is heavily penalized.

Community college entrants earn less and are in less prestigious occupations than four year college entrants even after taking into account years of education, sex, race, work experience, socioeconomic background, ability, region, marital status and college goal. The average status of four year college entrants jobs is 12 points higher on the Duncan index than community college entrants. The effect of additional years of education is more important in understanding occupational differences for community than four year college entrants. This reflects, in part, the negative effect dropping out of a community college has on occupational status attainment. Starting one's higher education at a community college impacts adult socioeconomic status regardless of years of education completed.

Human capital theory centers on the importance of education in shaping adult earning ability. However, human capital theorists have not focused on how the differentiation of higher education into sectors affects earning ability. Both type of education as well as years of education are important in analyzing adult socioeconomic status. How the introduction of a two tiered higher educational system in the United States impacts adult status attainment is an area that is wide open for researchers to investigate.

TOWARDS A CONFLICT THEORY OF EDUCATIONAL ATTAINMENT AND LABOR MARKET OUTCOMES

My findings lend support to a conflict theory of educational experience and labor market outcomes. My works shows that African Americans and women are hurt more than white men, in terms of adult earning ability, by first entering a community than a four year college. Men benefit more than others in terms of occupational prestige by entering a four year college than a community college. Community colleges, I believe, magnify the effects of social class background and ability on educational attainment and adult socioeconomic status attainment. These differences are important too in light of the fact that 'nontraditional' students are over-represented in the community college population.

The tracking of nontraditional students, namely women, minorities, those from lower socioeconomic class backgrounds, and those who score lower on IQ type tests into community colleges is self-validating in that it manufactures the differences which justify it in the first place. The community college offers success for some, who may have performed well at a four year college or university; for others, it institutionalizes failure. It is critically important to better understand why community college entrance, compared to four year college entrance, has a deleterious effect on adult socioeconomic attainment.

The economic return to entering a four year college is greater than the return to entering a community college every thing else the same. A community college entrant with the same amount of education as a four year college entrant will earn less all else equal. Human capital theorists maintain that this is because the community college entrant's educational investment is not as valuable as is the four year entrant. In the examine I outlined above, data show that four year college entrants gain much more than the opportunity cost involved in entering a four year college. One cannot assume that should prospective community college entrants understand that community college education is a poor economic investment that they would enter instead a four year college or university. Many community college entrants cannot afford this option. Even if one examines the long term economic consequences of the college choice, the immediate cost of entering a four year college instead of a community college may not be a possible option for some. Those who can afford to send their children to a four year college, or those who pay for such an education themselves, enjoy a substantial benefit in adult earning ability. Educational aid and loan programs exist to help those people who cannot finance a college education on their own the opportunity to enter the higher educational system. These programs provide nontraditional students the opportunity to try to succeed via the educational institution. When such programs are cutback financially, such cuts help reinforce existing class divisions within higher education. For now, four year colleges provide an education for those who can afford to pay the price. Those who cannot afford this option will enter community colleges in even larger numbers, or no college at all, thereby giving them the illusion that they had a fair chance to try. Commuity college entrance has a deleterious impact, compared to four year college entrance, on college completion. Community college entrants who acquire the bachelor's degree do not realize the same return on their educational investment as will a four year college entrant. In the short or long run view, community colleges are not an advantageous place to begin a higher education. The differentiation of higher education into sectors supports, no alleviates, racial, sexual, and class divisions within the United States labor market.

It should be more widely recognized what the possible consequences are from first entering a community college rather than a four year college or university. Given this information, at least people could make an informed decision as regards the college choice. Perhaps, the community college system could better fill the niche in education for vocational programs. This would then be an option for those who wanted to pursue this kind of training. The basic problem with the community college is that it is generally perceived as a transfer oriented institution. Most community college students, though, drop out of college. On the other hand, the majority of four year college entrants complete the bachelor's degree. Community college do not just offer the first two years of a college education. They offer a different kind of education.

Commuity college entrance hurts most those it was supposedly established to serve. If we are serious about equal educational opportunity, all students should have the opportunity to begin their higher education at the same type of institution. Hierarchies within types of institutions will always exist. However, with the introduciton of the community college, we have a two tiered higher educational system. This is hierarchy within hierarchy. The differentiation of higher education into sectors has crreated a class based two tiered educational system. Community colleges are institutions of higher education for nontraditional students. On the other hand, four year colleges are for those students from higher socioeconomic backgrounds who can finance such an education. To track nontraditional students into community colleges reduces educational and career competition between community and four year college entrants. Is this a goal we aim to achieve?

Should our goal be equality of educational opportunity, it would be better served by open admission to four year colleges than by the burgeoning community college system. The creation of community colleges to give primarily nontraditional students the impression they had a chance to try is problematic in a society that stresses the democratic nature of its opportunity structure. Community colleges offer a different kind of college education. Four year colleges did not open their doors to the masses. Instead, community colleges emerged to handle the pressure for increased college enrollemnts in the 1960s. Once again, however, separate education is not equal education.

Higher education is critical education at least in regards to the determination of adult socioeconomic status. Further, one learns how to think critically. Who decides, though, who is capable of being educated? Who is educable? Community college entrants are generally perceived as less capable and less intelligent, as measured by standardized ability tests, than four year college entrants. If we dismiss community college students as being uneducable, then the community college system would not be so problematic. But, to dismiss so many as failures, to institutionalize their failure; to track other community college entrants into vocational programs, which are more in line with their social class background, then we too have failed. To ignore the needs of millions by tracking them into second class educational institutions is the loss of the soicety as a whole. We must continue to examine social barriers people face, especially problems faced by women, minorities, and those from lower socioeconomic backgrounds. We must examine structural and background factors that bear on their educational success and life chances. To dismiss these individuals as not deserving, or not capable of being educated, is to destroy the hearts and minds of many.

Today, there are some new programs that may shape the fate of the community college system. First, some four year colleges have entered into agreements with community colleges to accept the work of an associate's degree as meeting the general education requirements at the four year college or unviersity. These are sometimes called two plus two programs. Two years at a community college, then two years to finish at a four year college. A student must still take the major and minor electives and possibly some college requirements as well. Still there is less duplication and difficulty in transferring than when no such agreement holds. This agreement only works if the student took a transfer oriented program. Other degrees two year college students may acquire would not apply in this situation. Therefore, if one received a degree in a vocational field, the tranfer equivalency process would not hold for them. Such policies avoid the necessity of a person, usually in the registrar's office, from going through another's transcript and deciding, on a course by course basis, what counts for what. Typically students lose a lot of credits in this process. While their work may count for hours completed, they still need a lot of specific courses at the four year college or university. Undoubtedly, this creates much frustration. Further, there is typically a lot more time an individual must invest before they acquire the bachelor's degree.

Another program that may impact the commuity college system is the idea of distance learning. Increasing numbers of four year schools are providing distance learning opportunities for students all over the United States. This can be in the form of an on-air class or an internet class. These classes may well fill the same niche in higher education as the community college system presently does. If an entire program is offered via distance education, a student may pursue this as an option rather than entering a community college then transferring to a four year college or university. How the impact of distance learning will shape the entire world of higher education is something that will be of interest to watch.

Appendix A

Methodology

The data for this work comes from a sample selected from the two youth cohorts of the National Longitudinal Survey of Labor Market Experience (NLS) and the National Longitudinal Survey of Youth (NLSY) which has been carried out by Herbert Parnes and his associates at Ohio State University. The initial sample year for the NLS sample of young men was 1966; for young women, 1968. The National Longitudinal Survey of Youth consists of 12,686 people who were 14-21 years old in 1979. The respondents in the NLSY have been interviewed every year since 1979 and we currently have data through 1990. The retention of the NLSY is high; 82 percent of the original respondents were surveyed in 1990.

The survey was funded by the United States Department of Labor. The Bureau of the Census drew the samples, conducted interviews, and processed the data. The Center for the Study of Human Resources at Ohio State University designed the interview schedules. The researchers obtained virtually all questionnaire information directly from the respondents. Among the NLS my sample includes those who have been out of high school exactly ten years, are working full time (35 or more hours per week), and who have IQ scores available. Among the NLSY, my sample includes all those who graduated from high school and are working full time.

The sample of young men and women holding a full time job ten years after high school graduation consists of 1,494 and 631 people, respectively. Respondents without information on IQ or who were enrolled in school full time were excluded. Since my sample consists of full time workers, respondents who never worked, were unemployed, working part time, or who were unable to work were also excluded. The entire sample of young men and women (NLS sample) consists of 2,125 individuals.

Limiting the sample to those who have IQ scores should not bias my estimates of the returns to schooling for this data set since data on IQ are missing almost at random.[1] Because all the individuals in my sample (from the NLS) have been out of high school ten year, their age is not that variable. The mean age from this sample is 27. Since age is a significant variable in analyzing adult earning ability, my analysis must be viewed with the knowledge that age is not an explanatory variable in this work.

Two of the dependent variables in my work are log adjusted hourly wage and occupational status. Since I am using longitudinal data, it is necessary to adjust wages so that comparisons can be made between years. The adjustment is made by the use of an index number which adjusts for inflation and productivity. The index was constructed from the total gross average hourly earning of production or non-supervisory workers on private payrolls. This information was taken from the Employment and Training Report of the President. The adjusted wage is a ratio of an individual's hourly wage in a given year divided by the index number for the same year. I use log adjusted hourly wage so that I can estimate the percentage increase in earnings associated with each independent variable. Logarithmic coefficients between 0 and .10 closely approximate percentage effects. Thus, for small changes in a given independent variable the logarithmic coefficient will always equal the percentage effect; for large changes the logarithmic coefficient will always underestimate the percentage effect.[2]

The Duncan Socioeconomic index of occupational status is used to define differences in occupational status by level and kind of education when utilizing regression analysis. An occupations Duncan score is based on the percentage of men working in the occupation who had completed high school and the percentage with incomes of $3,500 or more in 1950.[3] The Duncan score ranges between 0 to 96. In my descriptive analysis, I categorize occupations into three broad groups. These groups include: blue collar, white collar, and professional or managerial workers.

This procedure was utilized in order to simplify presentation of the data for the purpose of a descriptive analysis.

In analyzing the odds of entering a community college rather than a four year college and the likelihood of acquisition of the bachelor's degree, the dependent variables are dichotomous in nature. This violates assumptions of ordinary least squares regression analysis. Therefore, logistic analysis was chosen because it provides the power of regression analysis and yields parameters that enable the estimation of the effects of independent variables on the odds of a dichotomous dependent variable.[4] In this model, the regression parameters indicate a unit change in the log of the odds of community college entrance or acquisition of the bachelor's degree. The additive coefficients (b) were transformed to their multiplicative counterparts (e^b). Focusing on multiplicative effects eases interpretation by removing the logarithm from both sides of the equation. This allows one to analyze the effect of a unit change in the independent variable on the odds of falling into category one of the dependent variable. The dependent variables in this study are entering a community college or not; and acquisition of the bachelor's degree or not. An odds ratio greater than 1.0 indicates an increased likelihood of community college entrance/bachelor's degree acquisition, while an odds ratio less than 1.0 indicates a decreased likelihood of the event occurring. Thus the direction of an odds ratio, whether it is greater or less than 1.0, "can be thought of as its "sign"".[5]

Several independent variables in the model merit further discussion. Work experience, for young men, was calculated by subtracting years of education plus five from their age. This is limited to experience occurring after the age of 16. This is a commonly used construct for the work experience variable. Since it is not as socially necessary for women to work outside the home it is necessary to take into account non-work time in calculating their work experience. For young women, experience was calculated by subtracting years of education plus 5 and non work experience from their age. Non-work experience was calculated for all yeas after the completion of schooling.

Parental socioeconomic status is the equally weighted sum of the respondents father's education, father's occupational status when the respondent was 14, educational attainment of the oldest older sibling, and a measure of the availability of reading material in the home when the respondent was 14. The normalized socioeconomic status variable has a mean of 0 and a standard deviation of 1.

Educational attainment is measured by years of schooling completed. Type of first college entered is a dummy variable. If the respondent first entered a four year college, they received a score of 1; 0 otherwise. IQ scores were obtain from the first high school the respondent attended.

Region is a dummy variable that distinguishes respondents who live outside the South from all others. Southern states include: Delaware, Maryland, the District of Columbia, Virginia, West Virginia, North Carolina, South Carolina, Georgia, Florida, Kentucky, Tennessee, Alabama, Mississippi, Arkansas, Louisiana, Oklahoma, and Texas. I also examined the effect on adult socioeconomic status of living in a standard metropolitan statistical area or not.

Educational goal was defined as whether or not the respondent wanted to attain at least a bachelor's degree or not. This was a dummy variable. Marital status was coded as a dummy variable. Respondents were divided between those who were currently married compared to those who were not.

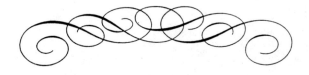

ENDNOTES

Chapter 1. Community College in the Higher Educational System.

1. Pincus, Fred. "The False Promises of Community Colleges: Class Conflict and Vocational Education." *Harvard Educational Review*, 50, 1980; Touraine, Alain. The Academic System in American Society. New York: McGraw-Hill Book Company, 1974.

2. Fields, R.R. The Community College Movement. New York: McGraw Hill, 1988; Hurlburt, Allan. "Community Colleges, Dream and Reality." *Community College Review*, 16, 1988.

3. Garms, Walter I. *Financing Community Colleges*. New York: Teachers College Press, 1977.

4. Breneman, David and Susan Nelson. *Financing Community Colleges*. Washington, DC: The Brookings Institution, 1981.

5. Grubb, W. Norton. "The Effects of Differentiation on Educational Attainment: The Case of Community Colleges." *The Review of Higher Education*, 12, 1989.

6. Medsker, Leland and Dale Tillery. *Breaking the Access Barriers: A Profile of Two-Year Colleges*. New York: McGraw-Hill Books, 1971.

7. Lloyd, Cynthia B., and Beth Niemi. *The Economics of Sex Differentials*. New York: Columbia University Press, 1979.

8. Karabel, Jerome. "Community Colleges and Social Stratification." *Harvard Educational Review*, 42, 1972; Dougherty, Kevin. "The Community College at the Crossroads: The Need for Structural Reform." *Harvard Educational Review*, 61, 1991.

9. Bowles, Samuel and Herbert Gintis. "Schooling and Inequality from Generation to Generation." *Journal of Political Economy*, 80, 1972.

10. United States Department of Education. *National Center for Education Statistics*. Washington, DC: U.S. Government Printing Office, 1996.

11. United States Department of Education. *National Center for Education Statistics*. Washington, DC: U.S. Government Printing Office, 1995.

12. Monk-Turner, Elizabeth and Yoko Baba. "Gender and College Opportunities: Changes Over Time in the United States and Japan." *Sociological Inquiry*, 57, 1987.

13. United States Department of Education. *National Center for Education Statistics*. Washington, DC: U.S. Government Printing Office, 1996.

14. United States Department of Education. *National Center for Education Statistics*. Washington, DC: U.S. Government Printing Office, 1996.

15. Ballantine, Jeanne H. *The Sociology of Education*. Englewood Cliffs, NJ: Prentice Hall, 1993.

16. United States Department of Education. *National Center for Education Statistics*. Washington, DC: U.S. Government Printing Office, 1996.

17. Dougherty, Kevin. "The Effects of Community Colleges: Aid or Hindrance to Socioeconomic Attainment?" *Sociology of Education*, 60, 1987.
18. Spurr, Stephen H. *Academic Degree Structures: Innovative Approaches.* New York: McGraw-Hill Book Company, 1970.
19. Brint, Steven and Jerome Karabel. *The Diverted Dream.* Oxford: Oxford University Press, 1989; Link, Charles and Edward Ratledge. "Social Returns to the Quantity and Quality of Schooling." *Journal of Human Resources*, 10, 1975.
20. Karabel, Jerome and Alexander Astin. "Social Class, Academic Ability and College 'Quality'." *Social Forces*, 53, 1975.
21. Valez, William. "Finishing College: The Effects of College Type." *Sociology of Education*, 58, 1985; Medsker, Leland and J.W. Trent. *The influence of different types of public higher institutions on college attendance from varying socioeconomic and ability levels.* Berkeley: Center for Research and Development in Higher Education, 1964.
22. Valez, William. "Finishing College: The Effects of College Type." *Sociology of Education*, 58, 1985.
23. Lee, Valerie, C. Mackie-Lewis and Helen Marks. "Persistence to the Baccalaureate Degree for Students who Transfer from Community College." *American Journal of Education*, 102, 1993.
24. United States Department of Education. *The Condition of Education (1997).* Washington, DC: U.S. Government Printing Office, 1997.

Chapter 2. Functional and Conflict Theories of Educational Experience and Labor Market Outcomes.

1. Merton, Robert. *Social Theory and Social Structure.* New York: The Free Press, 1968.
2. Van den Berghe, P. "Dialectic and Functionalism: Towards a Theoretical Synthesis." *American Sociological Review*, 28, 1963.
3. Halsey, A.H., Jean Floud, and C. Arnold Anderson (eds.). *Education, Economy and Society.* New York: The Free Press, 1961.
4. Karabel, Jerome and A.H. Halsey. *Power and Ideology in Education.* New York: Oxford University Press, 1977.
5. Becker, Gary S. *Human Capital.* New York: National Bureau of Economic Research, 1964; Schultz, Theodore W. *The Economic Value of Education.* New York: Columbia University Press, 1963.
6. Karabel, Jerome and A.H. Halsey. *Power and Ideology in Education.* New York: Oxford University Press, 1977.
7. Davis, Kingsley and Wilbert Moore. "Some Principles of Stratification." *American Sociological Review*, 10, 1945.
8. Johnson, George E. And Frank Stafford. "Social Returns to Quantity and Quality of Schooling." *Journal of Human Resources*, 8, 1973.

9. Freeman, Richard. *The Over-Educated American*. New York: Academic Press, 1976.

10. Spence, Michael. *Signaling and Screening*. HIER. Discussion Paper #467. Cambridge, MA: Harvard University, 1976.

11. Medina, Esteban. "University and the Labor Market." *Revista Espanola de Investigaciones Sociologicas*, 24, 1983.

12. Porter, Marion. "John Porter and Education: Technical Functionalist or Conflict Theorist." *Canadian Review of Sociology and Anthropology*, 18, 1981.

13. Liebow, Elliot. *Tally's Corner*. Boston: Little, Brown and Company, 1967.

14. Kuhn, Thomas S. *The Structure of Scientific Revolutions*. Second Edition. Chicago: The University of Chicago Press, 1970.

15. Gouldner, Alvin. *The Coming Crisis of Western Sociology*. New York: Avon Books, 1970.

16. Coser, Lewis A. *The Functions of Social Conflict*. New York: The Free Press, 1956.

17. Addison, John T. And W. Stanley Siebert. *The Market for Labor: An Analytical Treatment*. California: Goodyear Publishing Company, Inc., 1979.

18. Folbre, Nancy and Heidi Hartmann. "The Rhetoric of Self-Interest: Ideology and Gender in Economic Theory." In Arjo Klamer, Donald McCloskey and Robert Solow (eds.). The *Consequences of Economic Rhetoric*. New York: Cambridge University Press.

19. Pincus, Fred. "The False Promises of Community Colleges: Class Conflict and Vocational Education." *Harvard Educational Review*, 50, 1980.

20. Karabel, Jerome and Katherine McCelland. "Occupational Advantage and the Impact of College Rank on Labor Market Outcomes." *Sociological Inquiry*, 57, 1987.

21. Karabel, Jerome. "Community Colleges and Social Stratification." *Harvard Educational Review*, 42, 1972..

22. Bowles, Samuel and Herbert Gintis. *Schooling in Capitalist America*. Educational Reform and the Contradictions of Economic Life. New York: Basic Books, 1976.

23. Berg, Ivar. *Education and Jobs: The Great Training Robbery*. New York: Praeger, 1970.

24. Clark, Burton R. "The Cooling-Out Function in Higher Education." *American Journal of Sociology*, 65, 1960.

25. Block, N.J. and Gerald Dworkin. *The IQ Controversy*. New York: Pantheon Books, 1976.

26. Marx, Karl. *Wage-Labour and Capital*. New York: International Publishers, 1971.

27. Sewell, William H. And Robert M. Hauser. *Education, Occupations, and Earnings.* New York: Academic Press, 1975.

28. Dougherty, Kevin. "The Effects of Community Colleges: Aid of Hindrance to Socioeconomic Attainment?" *Sociology of Education,* 60, 1987.

29. Bowles, Samuel and Herbert Gintis. *Schooling in Capitalist America.* Educational Reform and the Contradictions of Economic Life. New York: Basic Books, 1976.

30. Sarup, Madan. *Marxism and Education.* London: Routledge and Kegan Paul, 1978.

Chapter 3. Who Enters Community and Four Year Colleges? Who Acquires the Bachelor's Degree?

1. Alexander, Karl, Scott Holupka and Aaron Passas. "Social Background and Academic Determinants of Two-Year verus Four-Year College Attendance: Evidence from Two Cohorts a Decade Apart." *American Journal of Education,* 96, 1987.

2. Fact Book 1988-89 of Higher Education in Virginia. Virginia, 1988-1989.

3. Komarovsky, Mirra. *Women in College.* New York: Basic Books, 1985.

4. Alba, Richard and David Lavin. "Community Colleges and Tracking in Higher Education." *Sociology of Education,* 54, 1981.

5. United States Department of Education. *The Condition of Education (1997).* Washington, D.C.: U.S. Government Printing Office, 1997.

Chapter 4. First College Entered, Occupational Status, and Gender.

1. Alwin, Duane F. "College effects on educational and occupational attainments." *American Sociological Review,* 39, 1974.

2. Pincus, Fred. "The false promises of community colleges: class conflict and vocational education." *Harvard Educational Review,* 50, 1980.

3. Karabel, Jerome. "Community colleges and social stratification." *Harvard Educational Review,* 42, 1972.

4. Freeman, Richard B. *The Over-Educated American.* New York: Academic Press, 1976.

5. Sewell, William H., Robert Hauser, and Wendy Wolf. "Sex, Schooling, and Occupational Status." *American Journal of Sociology,* 86, 1980.

Chapter 5. Economic Returns to Education: Do Rates of Return Vary Between Community and Four-Year College Entrants?

1. Mincer, Jacob. *Schooling, Experience, and Earnings.* New York: National Bureau of Economic Research, 1974.

2. Kane, Thomas and Cecilia Rouse. *"Labor Market Returns to Two- and Four-Year Colleges: Is a Credit a Credit and Do Degrees Matter?"* NBER Working Paper #4268. Cambridge, MA: NBER, 1993.

3. Ashenfelter, Orley and Alan Krueger. *"Estimates of the Economic Return to Schooling From a New Sample of Twins."* National Bureau of Economic Research. Working Paper #4143. Cambridge, MA: NBER, 1992.

4. Nolfi, George J., et al. *Experiences of Recent High School Graduates.* The Transition to Work or Post-secondary Education. Lexington, MA: Lexington Books, 1978.

5. Link, Charles and Edward Ratledge. "Social Returns to Quantity and Quality of Schooling." *Journal of Human Resources*, 10, 1975.

6. Becker, Gary S. *Human Capital.* New York: National Bureau of Economic Resarch, 1964.

7. Karabel, Jerome. "Community colleges and social stratification." *Harvard Educational Review*, 42, 1972.

8. Cohn, Elchanan. *The Economics of Education.* Cambridge, MA: Ballinger Publishing Company, 1979.

9. Breneman, David W. And Susan C. Nelson. *Financing Community Colleges.* An Economic Perspective. Washington, DC: The Brookings Institution, 1981.

10. Lee, Valerie and Kenneth Frank. "Students' Characteristics That Facilitate the Transfer from Two Year to Four Year Colleges." *Sociology of Education*, 63, 1990.

11. United States Department of Education. *Conditions of Education.* Washington, DC: U.S. Government Printing Office, 1997.

Chapter 6. Another Look at the Economic Return to Education and Degrees.

1. This chapter is based on a working paper titled "The Returns to Education and Degrees" with C.G. Turner.

2. Alwin, Duane. "College Effects on Educational and Occupational Attainments." *American Sociological Review*, 39, 1974.

3. Monk-Turner, Elizabeth. "Economic Returns to Community and Four Year College Education." *Journal of Socio-Economics*, 23, 1994.

4. Kane, Thomas J. And Cecilia Rouse. *"Labor Market Returns to Two- and Four-Year Colleges: Is a Credit a Credit and Do Degrees Matter?"* Cambridge, MA: National Bureau of Economic Research, Inc., 1993.

5. Jaeger, David A. and Marianne Page. "Degrees Matter: New Evidence on Sheepskin Effects in the Returns to Education." *Review of Economics and Statistics*, 78, 1996.

6. Spence, Michael. *Signaling and Screening.* HIER. Discussion Paper #467. Cambridge, MA: Harvard University, 1976.

7. They were 27 years old in 1988.

8. Kominski, Robert and Andrea Adams. *School Enrollment--Social and Economic Characteristics of Students: October 1991*. Washington, DC: Department of Commerce, 1993.

9. United States Department of Education. Bureau of Labor Statistics. Employment Status of School Age Youth, High School Graduates and Dropouts. Washington, DC: U.S. Government Printing Office, 1993.

10. United States Department of Labor. Bureau of Labor Statistics. *Employment Status of School Age Youth, High School Graduates and Dropouts*. Washington, DC: U.S. Government Printing Office, 1993.

11. Wonnacott, Michael. *Apprenticeship and the Future of the Work Force*. ERIC Digest #124. Columbus, Ohio: ERIC Clearinghouse on Adult, Career, and Vocational Education, 1992.

12. Briggs, Vernon and F. Foltman (eds.). *Apprenticeship Research: Emerging Findings and Future Trends*. Ithaca, NY: School of Industrial and Labor Relations at Cornell University, 1981.

13. Reich, Robert. "Beyond the politics of preservation: the Clinton administration's workforce strategy." Remarks to the Center for National Policy's Newsmaker Luncheon. Unpublished paper, 1993.

14. United States Department of Labor. Bureau of Labor Statistics. *Employment Status of School Age Youth, High School Graduates and Dropouts*. Washington, DC: U.S. Government Printing Office, 1993.

15. United States Department of Labor. Bureau of Labor Statistics. *Employment Status of School Age Youth, High School Graduates and Dropouts*. Washington, DC: U.S. Government Printing Office, 1993.

16. Berheide, Catherine. "Women in Sales and Service Occupations." In A. H. Stromberg and S. Harkess (eds.). *Women Working*. Mountain View, CA: Mayfield Publishing Company, 1988.

17. Reich, Robert. "Beyond the politics of preservation: the Clinton administration's workforce strategy." Remarks to the Center for National Policy's Newsmaker Luncheon. Unpublished Paper, 1993.

18. Bound, John and Richard Freeman. "What Went Wrong? The Erosion of Relative Earnings and Employment Among Young Black Men in the 1980's." *Quarterly Journal of Economics*, 107, 1992.

19. Dougherty, Kevin. "The Effects of Community Colleges: Aid or Hindrance to Socioeconomic Attainment?" *Sociology of Education*, 60, 1987; Karabel, Jerome. "Community Colleges and Social Stratification." *Harvard Educational Review*, 42, 1972; Valez, William. "Finishing College: The Effects of College Type." *Sociology of Education*, 58, 1985.

20. Mincer, J. *Schooling, Experience, and Earnings*. New York: National Bureau of Economic Research, 1974; Sewell, W.H. and Robert Hauser. *Education, Occupation, and Earnings*. New York: Academic Press, 1975.

21. These are estimated expected returns.

22. Cohn, E. *The Economics of Education*. Cambridge, MA: Ballinger, 1979.

23. United States Department of Labor. Bureau of Labor Statistics. Washington, DC: U.S. Government Printing Office, 1996.
24. United States Department of Labor. Bureau of Labor Statistics. Washington, DC: U.S. Government Printing Office, 1996.
25. Karoly, Lynn A. "Changes in the distribution of individual earnings in the United States: 1967-1986." *Review of Economics and Statistics*, 74, 1992.
26. Goldin, Claudia. *Understanding the Gender Gap*. New York: Oxford University Press, 1990.
27. Neumark, David and Michele McLennan. "Sex Discrimination and Women's Labor Market Outcomes." *The Journal of Human Resources*, 30, 1995.
28. Monk-Turner, Elizabeth. "The Occupational Achievements of Community and Four Year College Entrants." *American Sociological Review*, 55, 1990.

Chapter 7. Community College Entrance: Better Than Not Going to College at All?

1. This chapter is based on a working paper titled "Is Going to a Community College Better than not Going to College at All?" with C.G. Turner.
2. Alwin, Duane F. "College effects on educational and occupational attainments." The *American Sociological Review*, 1, 1974.
3. Zwerling, L. Steven. *Second Best*. New York: McGraw Hill, 1976.
4. Community college entrants include all students who first entered a community college, rather than a four year institutions, regardless of their educational outcomes. Educational outcomes are used as control variables.
5. United States Department of Labor. *Statistical Abstract of the United States*.Washington, DC: U.S. Government Printing Office, 1990.
6. United States Department of Education. *Center for Education Statistics*. "Fall Enrollment in Colleges and Universities." Washington, DC: U.S. Government Printing Office, 1988.
7. Spence, Michael. "Signaling and Screening." HIER. Discussion Paper #467. Cambridge, MA Harvard University, 1976.
8. Tinto, V. "The Distribution Effects of Public Junior College Availability." *Research in Higher Education*, 1, 1975.
9. Pincus, Fred. "The False Promises of Community Colleges: Class Conflict and Vocational Education." *Harvard Educational Review*, 1, 1980.
10. Brint, Steven and Jerome Karabel. *The Diverted Dream*. Oxford: Oxford University Press, 1989.
11. Grubb, W. Norton. "Correcting Conventional Wisdom: Community College Impact on Students' Jobs and Salaries." *Community, Technical, and Junior College Journal*, 1, 1992.
12. Ryan, P.B. "Why Industry Needs the Junior College." In W.K. Ogilvie

114

and M.R. Raines (eds.). *Perspectives on the Community Junior College.* New York: Appleton Century Crofts, 1971.

13. Levy, Frank and Richard Murnane. "U.S. Earnings Levels and Earnings Inequality: A Review of Recent Trends and Proposed Explanations." *Journal of Economic Literature*, 1, 1992.

14. Sewell, William H., Robert Hauser, and Wendy Wolf. "Sex, Schooling, and Occupational Status." *American Journal of Sociology*, 86, 1980.

15. Velez, William. "Finishing College: The Effect of College Type." *Sociology of Education*, 1, 1985.

16. Link, Charles and Edward Ratledge. "Social Returns to Quantity and Quality of Schooling." *Journal of Human Resources*, 1, 1975.

17. Freeman, Richard. *The Over-Educated American.* New York: Academic Press, 1976.

18. Blau, Peter and Otis Dudley Duncan. *The American Occupational Structure.* New York: Wiley and Sons, 1967; Featherman, David L. and Robert Hauser. *The Process of Stratification.* Trends and Analysis. New York: The Academic Press, 1977.

Conclusion.

1. Karabel, Jerome. "Community Colleges and Social Stratification." *Harvard Educational Review*, 42, 1972.

2. Valez, William. "Finishing College: The Effects of College Type." *Sociology of Education*, 58, 1985.1997

3. United States Department of Education. *The Condition of Education (1997).* Washington, DC: U.S. Government Printing Office, 1997.

4. Clark, Burton R. "The Cooling-Out Function in Higher Education." *American Journal of Sociology*, 65, 1960.

Appendix A. Methodology.

1. Griliches, Zvi. "Estimating the Returns to Schooling: Some Econometric Problems." *Econometrica*, 45, 1977.

2. Morgan, Philip and Jay Teachman. "Logistic Regression: Description, Examples, and Comparisons." *Journal of Marriage and the Family*, 50, 1990.

3. Duncan, Otis Dudley. "A Socioeconomic Index for all Occupations." In Albert Reiss, Jr. (Ed.) *Occupations and Social Status.* New York: The Free Press, 1961.

4. Morgan, Philip and Jay Teachman. "Logistic Regression: Description, Examples, and Comparisons." *Journal of Marriage and the Family*, 50, 1990.

5. Morgan, Philip and Jay Teachman. "Logistic Regression: Description, Examples, and Comparisons." *Journal of Marriage and the Family*, 50, 1990.

BIBLIOGRAPHY

Addison, John T. and W. Stanley Siebert. *The Market for Labor: An Analytical Treatment*. California: Goodyear Publishing Company, Inc., 1979.

Alba, Richard and David Lavin. "Community Colleges and Tracking in Higher Education." *Sociology of Education*, 54, 1981.

Alexander, Karl, Scott Holupka and Aaron Passas. "Social Background and Academic Determinants of Two-Year versus Four-year College Attendance: Evidence from Two Cohorts a Decade Apart." *American Journal of Education*, 96, 1987.

Alwin, Duane F. "College effects on educational and occupational attainments." *American Sociological Review*, 39, 1974.

Ashenfelter, Orley and Alan Krueger. "Estimates of the Economic Return to Schooling From A New Sample of Twins." *National Bureau of Economic Research*. Working Paper #4143. Cambridge, MA: NBER, 1992.

Ballantine, Jeanne H. *The Sociology of Education*. Englewood Cliffs, NJ: Prentice Hall, 1993.

Becker, Gary S. *Human Capital*. New York: National Bureau of Economic Research, 1964.

Berg, Ivar. *Education and Jobs: The Great Training Robbery*. New York: Praeger, 1970.

Berheide, Catherine. "Women in Sales and Service Occupations." In A.H. Stromberg and S. Harkess (eds.). *Women Working*. Mountain View, CA: Mayfield Publishing Company, 1988.

Blau, Peter and Otis Dudley Duncan. *The American Occupational Structure*. New York: Wiley and Sons, 1967.

Block, N.J. and Gerald Dworkin. *The IQ Controversy*. New York: Pantheon Books, 1976.

Bound, John and Richard Freeman. "What Went Wrong? The Erosion of Relative Earnings And Employment Among Young Black Men in the 1980's." *Quarterly Journal of Economics*, 107, 1992.

Bowles, Samuel and Herbert Gintis. "Schooling and Inequality from Generation to Generation." *Journal of Political Economy*, 80, 1972.

Bowles, Samuel and Herbert Gintis. *Schooling in Capitalist America*. New York: Basic Books, 1976.

Breneman, David and Susan Nelson. *Financing Community Colleges*. Washington, DC: The Brooking Institution, 1981.

Briggs, Vernon and F. Foltman (eds.). *Apprenticeship Research: Emerging Findings and Future Trends*. Ithaca. NY: School of Industrial and Labor Relations at Cornell University, 1981.

Brint, Steven and Jerome Karabel. *The Diverted Dream*. Oxford: Oxford University Press, 1989.

Clark, Burton R. "The Cooling-Out Function in Higher Education." *American Journal of Sociology,* 65, 1960.

Cohn, Elchanan. *The Economics of Education.* Cambridge, MA: Ballinger Publishing Company, 1979.

Coser, Lewis A. *The Functions of Social Conflict.* New York: The Free Press, 1956.

Davis, Kingsley and Wilbert Moore. "Some Principles of Stratification." *American Sociological* Review, 10, 1945.

Dougherty, Kevin. "The Effects of Community Colleges: Aid or Hindrance to Socioeconomic Attainment?" *Sociology of Education,* 60, 1987.

Dougherty, Kevin. "The Community college at the Crossroads: The Need for Structural Reform." *Harvard Educational Review,* 61, 1991.

Duncan, Otis Dudley. "A Socioeconomic Index for all Occupations." In Albert Reiss, Jr. (Ed.). *Occupations and Social Status.* New York: The Free Press, 1961.

Fact Book 1988-89 of Higher Education in Virginia. Virginia, 1988-1989.

Featherman, David L. and Robert Hauser. *The Process of Stratification.* Trends and Analysis. New York: The Academic Press, 1977.

Fields, R.R. *The Community College Movement.* New York: McGraw Hill, 1988.

Folbre, Nancy and Heidi Hartmann. "The Rhetoric of Self-Interest: Ideology and Gender in Economic Theory." In Arjo Klamer, Donald McCloskey and Robert Solow (eds.). *The Consequences of Economic Rhetoric.* New York: Cambridge University Press.

Freeman, Richard. *The Over-Educated American.* New York: Academic Press, 1976.

Garms, Walter I. *Financing Community Colleges.* New York: Teachers College Press, 1977.

Goldin, Claudia. *Understanding the Gender Gap.* New York: Oxford University Press, 1990.

Gouldner, Alvin. *The Coming Crisis of Western Sociology.* New York: Avon Books, 1970.

Griliches, Zvi. "Estimating the Returns to Schooling: Some Econometric Problems." *Econometrica,* 45, 1977.

Grubb, W. Norton. "The Effects of Differentiation on Educational Attainment: The Case of Community Colleges." *The Review of Higher Education,* 12, 1989.

Grubb, W. Norton. "Correcting Convention Wisdom: Community College Impact on Students' Jobs and Salaries." *Community, Technical, and Junior College Journal,* 1, 1992.

Halsey, A.H., Jean Floud, and C. Arnold Anderson (eds.). *Education, Economy and Society.* New York: The Free Press, 1961.

Jaeger, David A. and Marianne Page. "Degrees Matter: New Evidence on Sheepskin Effect In the Returns to Education." *Review of Economics and Statistics*, 78, 1996.

Johnson, George E. and Frank Stafford. "Social Returns to Quantity and Quality of Schooling." *Journal of Human Resources*, 8, 1973.

Kane, Thomas and Cecilia Rouse. *"Labor Market Returns to Two- and Four-Year Colleges: Is a Credit a Credit and Do Degrees Matter?"* NBER Working Paper #4268. Cambridge, MA: NBER, 1993.

Karabel, Jerome. "Community Colleges and Social Stratification." *Harvard Educational Review*, 42, 1972.

Karabel, Jerome and Alexander Astin. "Social Class, Academic Ability and College 'Quality'." *Social Forces*, 53, 1975.

Karabel, Jerome and A.H. Halsey. *Power and Ideology in Education*. New York: Oxford University Press, 1977.

Karabel, Jerome and Katherine McClelland. "Occupational Advantage and the Impact of College Rank of Labor Market Outcomes." *Sociological Inquiry*, 57, 1987.

Karoly, Lynn A. "Changes in the distribution of individual earnings in the United States: 1967-1986." *Review of Economics and Statistics*, 74, 1992.

Komarovsky, Mirra. *Women in College*. New York: Basic Books, 1985.

Kominski, Robert and Andrea Adams. *School Enrollments--Social and Economics Characteristics of Students: October 1991*. Washington, DC: Department of Commerce, 1993.

Kuhn, Thomas S. *The Structure of Scientific Revolutions*. Second Edition. Chicago: The University of Chicago Press, 1970.

Lee, Valerie and Kenneth Frank. "Students' Characteristics That Facilitate the Transfer from Two Year to Four Year Colleges." *Sociology of Education*, 63, 1990.

Lee, Valerie, C. Mackie-Lewis and Helen Marks. "Persistence to the Baccalaureate Degree For Students who Transfer from Community College." *American Journal of Education*, 102, 1993.

Levy, Frank and Richard Murnane. "U.S. Earnings Levels and Earnings Inequality: A Review Of Recent Trends and Proposed Explanations." *Journal of Economic Literature*, 1, 1992.

Liebow, Elliot. *Tally's Corner*. Boston: Little, Brown and Company, 1967.

Link, Charles and Edward Ratledge. "Social Returns to the Quantity and Quality of Schooling." *Journal of Human Resources*, 10, 1975.

Lloyd, Cynthia B., and Beth Niemi. *The Economics of Sex Differentials*. New York: Columbia University Press, 1979.

Marx, Karl. *Wage-Labour and Capital*. New York: International Publishers, 1971.

Mincer, Jacob. *Schooling, Experience, and Earnings*. New York: National Bureau of Economic Research, 1974.

Medina, Esteban. "University and the Labor Market." *Revista Espanola de Investigaciones Sociologicas*, 24, 1983.

Medsker, Leland and Dale Tillery. *Breaking the Access Barriers: A Profile of Two-Year Colleges.* New York: McGraw-Hill Books, 1971.

Medsker, Leland and J.W. Trent. *The influences of different types of public higher Institutions on college attendance from varying socioeconomic and ability levels.* Berkeley: Center for Research and Development in Higher Education, 1964

Merton, Robert. *Social Theory and Social Structure.* New York: The Free Press, 1968.

Mincer, J. *Schooling, Experience, and Earnings.* New York: National Bureau of Economic Research, 1974.

Monk-Turner, Elizabeth. "Economic Returns to Community and Four-Year College Education," *Journal of Socio-Economics*, 23, 1994.

Monk-Turner, Elizabeth. "The Occupational Achievements of Community and Four Year College Entrants." *American Sociological Review*, 55, 1990.

Monk-Turner, Elizabeth and Yoko Baba. "Gender and College Opportunities: Changes Over Time in the United States and Japan." *Sociological Inquiry*, 57, 1987.

Morgan, Philip and Jay Teachman. "Logistic Regression: Description, Examples, and Comparisons." *Journal of Marriage and the Family*, 50, 1990.

Neumark, David and Michele McLennan. "Sex Discrimination and Women's Labor Market Outcomes." *The Journal of Human Resources*, 30, 1995.

Nolfi, George J., et. Al. *Experiences of Recent High School Graduates. The Transition to Work or Post-secondary Education.* Lexington, MA: Lexington Books, 1978.

Pincus, Fred. "The False Promises of Community Colleges: Class Conflict and Vocational Education." *Harvard Educational Review*, 50, 1980.

Porter, Marion. "John Porter and Education: Technical Functionalist or Conflict Theorist." *Canadian Review of Sociology and Anthropology*, 18, 1981.

Reich, Robert. *"Beyond the politics of preservation: the Clinton administration's workforce Strategy."* Remarks to the Center for National Policy's Newsmaker Luncheon. Unpublished Paper, 1993.

Ryan, P.B. "Why Industry Needs the Junior College." In W.K. Ogilvie and M.R. Raines (eds.). *Perspectives on the Community Junior College.* New York: Appleton Century Crofts, 1971.

Sarup, Madan. *Marxism and Education.* London: Routledge and Kegan Paul, 1978.

Sewell, William H. and Robert M. Hauser. *Education, Occupations, and Earnings.* New York: Academic Press, 1975.

Schultz, Theodore W. *The Economic Value of Education.* New York: Columbia University Press, 1963.

Sewell, William H., Robert Hauser, and Wendy Wolf. "Sex, Schooling, and Occupational Status." *American Journal of Sociology*, 86, 1980.

Spence, Michael. *Signaling and Screening*. Harvard Institute of Economic Research. Discussion Paper #467. Cambridge, MA: Harvard University, 1976.

Spurr, Stephen H. *Academic Degree Structures: Innovative Approaches*. New York: McGraw-Hill Book Company, 1970.

Tinto, V. "The Distribution Effects of Public Junior College Availability." *Research in Higher Education*, 1, 1975.

United States Department of Education. *Center for Education Statistics*. "Fall Enrollment in Colleges and Universities." Washington, DC: U.S. Government Printing Office, 1988.

United States Department of Education. *National Center for Education Statistics*. Washington, DC: U.S. Government Printing Office, 1995.

United States Department of Education. *National Center for Education Statistics*. Washington, DC: U.S. Government Printing Office, 1996.

United States Department of Education. *The Condition of Education (1997)*. Washington, DC: U.S. Government Printing Office, 1997.

United States Department of Labor. Bureau of Labor Statistics. *Employment Status of School Age Youth, High School Graduates and Dropouts*. Washington, DC: U.S. Government Printing Office, 1993.

United States Department of Labor. *Bureau of Labor Statistics*. Washington, DC: U.S. Government Printing Office, 1996.

United States Department of Labor. *Statistical Abstract of the United States*. Washington, DC: U.S. Government Printing Office, 1990.

Valez, William. "Finishing College: The Effects of College Type." *Sociology of Education*, 58, 1985.

Van den Berghe, P. "Dialectic and Functionalism: Towards a Theoretical Synthesis." *American Sociological Review*, 28, 1963.

Wonnacott, Michael. *Apprenticeship and the Future of the Work Force*. ERIC Digest #124. Columbus, Ohio: ERIC Clearinghouse on Adult, Career, and Vocational Education, 1992.

Zwerling, L. Steven. *Second Best*. New York: McGraw Hill, 1976.

Index

MELLEN STUDIES IN EDUCATION